中英双语道德经
Bilingual Dao De Jing

原著：老子　（AUTHOR：LAOZI ˜500 B.C.）

译：　　乌鸦子 （TRANSLATOR：WU YA ZI　2018）

COMMON SENSE EDITION

©2018 by Wuyazi 乌鸦子

Published by: Sansudao Bilingual Classics

ISBN: **978-1-949167-00-9**
Printed in the USA
Website: 1
Email: sansudaoist@gmail.com

I dedicate this translation to

Lix and E.A.C.H.

目录 (Table of Contents)

Translator's Preface:

This translation was born of a side-by-side comparison book reports of two foundational texts: *Dao De Jing* vs. *The US Constitution*
URL: http://taolaw.blogspot.com/2017/04/meets-us-constitution-preamble.html

The two books, were separated by more than 2000 years, born on two different continents, conceived by two disparate cultural tradition. Yet they both laid the foundation and shared profound Truths.

It turned out that there is only one human history and only one human nature. In the process of comparison reading, I found many Chinese Americans and ABCs have not had a full exposure to *Dao De Jing*. Hence, this book is to bring a version of *Dao De Jing* in mostly original Chinese, Pin Yin and English translation together, side by side. I hope this translation will help Chinese Americans to reevaluate their ancient heritage, while adapting to the American culture.

Differences between Chinese and English texts make accurate translation impossible. Readers please keep the following differences in mind:
1) Chinese texts almost never differentiate plural/singularity. No ingrained past tense and present and future tense.
2) often omit the subjects; subjects and objects are also often confused.
3) Many Chinese characters map to one sound. Some map to several sounds.
4) Pronouns are often vague. Articles are rare. No male-female difference.
5) No punctuations in ancient Chinese texts. However, the natural break in the bamboo sticks (writing medium) may give a clue on when to stop. No capitalizations, no emphasis.
6) Double negatives (often marked out by translator in parenthesis and *italics*)
7) Chapter orders may be mixed up. Some sentences seemed mixed up with other chapters. Etc.

Disclaimer: I am not a scholar who guarantee correctness; I could not match the original author's originality, simplicity and elegance. I merely put out a sensible version of *Dao De Jing*, with (not quite perfectly correct) pinyin, with a sensible version of translation, with some whimsical personal notes. Side by side, in hope of sharing enlightenment.

In this work, i am inspired by XiaoHuiXiong, and he generously donated his pinyin-arranged edition for (unmodified) publication, though my final pinyin edition was independently developed, and may have contained more errors. https://konghaisg.files.wordpress.com/2013/02/e88081e5ad90e98193e5beb7e7bb8fe6b3a8e99fb3e78988.pdf
I am also indebted to Yang Peng, whose translation of Dao De Jing United Edition was based on newer archaeological discoveries since 1970s. URL: https://www.amazon.com/Dao-Jing-United-Version-Laozi/dp/1581771576/
I am also indebted to many websites with their own edition and translations in Chinese and English. I mostly used WangBi's version of *Dao De Jing* from 2000 years ago. Internet is the greatest thing since *Dao De Jing*. Their URLs:
http://daodejing.weilishi.org/
http://daodejing.org/
I want to express my gratitude to Qian Zuo(of *North American Economic Herald*). She and her team helped me format the English and Chinese side by side and adding Pinyin.

Finally, I want to thank my family for their patience and love. Without them, I would not have gone this direction.

My point of view is a little different, and as far as I could tell, mostly common sense and probably original.
May the Force be with it.

Wuyazi at Sansudao
三俗道乌鸦子
http://sansudao.com
3.1.2018 (errors in fixed on 1.12.2019)

第一章 道可道
dì yī zhāng dào kě dào

道可道，非常道；
dào kě dào fēi cháng dào

名可名，非常名。
míng kě míng fēi cháng míng

无名，天地之始；
wú míng tiān dì zhī shǐ

有名，万物之母。
yǒu míng wàn wù zhī mǔ

故常无，欲以观其妙；
gù cháng wú yù yǐ guān qí miào

常有，欲以观其徼。
cháng yǒu yù yǐ guān qí jiǎo

此两者，同出而异名，同谓
cǐ liǎng zhě tóng chū ér yì míng tóng wèi

之玄，玄之又玄，众妙之
zhī xuán xuán zhī yòu xuán zhòng miào zhī

门。
mén

Chapter 1. A Dao that could be Spoken of

A Dao that could be spoken of, is not the eternal Dao;
A Name that could be named, is not the eternal Name.
Without Name, thus began Heaven and Earth;

With Name, thus (became) the Mother of all things;
Therefore, often **without** (something), (we) intend to observe its Truth;
often **with** (something), (we) intend to observe its mysteries.
These two things (**with** and **without**), have the same origin but are differently named. Both are called Profound, the most Profound of Profound, the gate to Truth.

Notes:

There are many ways to understand Dao De Jing, through the lens of any system science, like computer science, medicine, engineering, political engineering. It could also be understood as a series of Question and Answer sessions between the author, weary historic scholar from the Zhou capital city and an interviewer, (according to legend), a provincial officer. The sessions probably took place in an outpost far away from the fading Zhou capital.

The Interviewer, a provincial customs officer asked: What is the Way for me to be promoted?
Laozi: A Way (Dao 道) that could be spoken of (道), is not the Eternal Way. (a pun, a paradox) 道可道，非常道。
The Interviewer, undaunted: Please tell us about the news of the famous names in the Zhou Capital?
Laozi: A Name that could be named, is not the Eternal Name. (a pun, a paradox) 名可名，非常名。

The author opened with paradoxes and puns, then continued to write one of the most unique books ever and since. A short cryptic work, of apparently no practical value, naming no names, yet laid foundation to a hundred schools of thoughts within 200 years of its existence.

Why so? We will find out.
故常无，欲以观其妙；常有，欲以观其徼，"Therefore, often **without** (something), (we) intend to observe its Truth; often **with** (something), (we)intend to observe its mysteries."
This passage should offer the clue. In a single chapter, Laozi moved from existential paradoxes to advocate a scientific method of experimenting **with/without** A/B testing, and then he kept going.

By the end of *Dao De Jing*, he had gone over historic cycles, system stability and resilience, Simplicity over complexity, neutrality principles, branches of government, error correction, social standards and metrics, government Interference, legal underpinnings, scientific methods, sustainability and more.

道：the Way, the road, speak of, how things work, the algorithms, enlightenment, Dao
常：unchanging, frequent, sustainable, eternal
名：Names, fame, titles, variables
玄：Profound Black
有：With
无：Without
徼：Mysteries
妙：Beautiful but has connotations of Truth

第二章 美之为美

dì èr zhāng měi zhī wéi měi

天下皆知美之为美，斯恶
tiān xià jiē zhī měi zhī wéi měi   sī è
已。
yǐ

皆知善之为善，斯不善已。
jiē zhī shàn zhī wéi shàn   sī bú shàn yǐ

故有无相生，难易相成，长
gù yǒu wú xiāng shēng   nán yì xiāng chéng   cháng

短相形，高下相倾，音声相
duǎn xiāng xíng   gāo xià xiāng qīng   yīn shēng xiāng

和，前后相随。
hé   qián hòu xiāng suí

是以圣人处无为之事，行不
shì yǐ shèng rén chù wú wéi zhī shì   háng bù

言之教。
yán zhī jiào

万物作焉而不辞，生而不
wàn wù zuò yān ér bù cí   shēng ér bù

有，为而不恃，功成而弗
yǒu   wéi ér bù shì   gōng chéng ér fú

居。
jū

夫唯弗居，是以不去。
fū wéi fú jū   shì yǐ bù qù

Chapter 2. Beauty's Standard

If all under Heaven conform to a beauty's standard, then they are ugly.

If all conform to a goodness's standard, then they are not good.
Therefore, **with** and **without** create each other, difficulty and ease complement each other, long and short compare with each other, high and low lean on each other, melody and voice melt into each other, front and back follow each other.
Therefore, the Sage serves without Interference, teaches without big talk.

(He) helps all things out without shirking responsibility, creates without possessiveness, governs without pride, he completes his mission without dwelling on his accomplishments.
By not dwelling on his accomplishments, the Sage is remembered.

Notes:

After a paradoxical opening, the author proceeded to overturn the audience' traditional standards such as beauty and goodness. Standardization and conformity tend to distort reality and to cause unintended consequences that reverberates throughout a system. Laozi returned to this problem again and again, in order to solve it. Many example dimensions of **with** and **without** from the previous chapter (difficulty vs ease, long vs short, high vs low, front vs back) are expounded here and further in later chapters.

Instead of traditional standards, the author started to build up his alternative approach, its "standard" bearer being the Sage (圣人), yet opposing standardization and conformity. These words were bold, revolutionary words, would have landed speaker into trouble anywhere else in the ancient world.

The Ancient China was a tolerant place, people like Laozi, Zhuangzi and Mozi, enjoyed natural life spans (unlike their Western counterparts, say, Socrates). The quality of their work was testimony to the ancient Chinese tradition of free speech.

圣人：Sage   功成：Mission complete

第三章 不尚贤

不尚贤，使民不争。

不贵难得之货，使民不为盗。

不见可欲，使民心不乱。

是以圣人之治，虚其心，实其腹，弱其志，强其骨；

常使民无知无欲，使夫智者不敢为也。

为无为，则无不治。

Chapter 3. Avoid Admiring the Virtuous

(The Sage) avoids admiring the virtuous, so people will not compare and compete.

(He) avoids treasuring the rare goods, so people will not rob.

(He) avoids displaying his own Preferences, so that people will not forget their own true Preferences.

Therefore, under the Sage's leadership, people's hearts are humble (and ready for Truth), their bellies are filled, their ambitions are moderate, their backbones are strengthened.

(The Sage) keeps his people without devious tricks and without ulterior motives, so that devious people dare not interfere.

If (he) avoids interfering, all is well regulated.

Notes:

The author Laozi continued to overturn the traditional virtues. The virtuous, the precious, the Interfering, the motivated, all became undesirables. These chapters were distinctly Daoist, as opposed to Confucian and Mohist thinking. Laozi, was a learned court historian, and an heir to 500+ years of Zhou and Shang Dynasty written history. He pointed out how, even apparently harmless pursuits, such as "virtues" and "goods" and "preferences", could still cause disastrous consequences when imposed or encouraged from the top.

Top down interference, complexity and conformity, are like Trojan Horses. They look beautiful, sound great, but in practice, they lull people into a false sense of security and then ambush their victims. The author advocated no government interference, Simplicity and Truth as protection against these enemies.

为：action, accomplishments. Laozi has a tendency of turning words with positive connotations negative, this word is an example. In Dao De Jing, this word often means interference, grandstanding, faking

无为：No-Interference, no apparent action, no action, no faking.

无知：No devious Tricks

无欲：No devious hidden motives, no desires

智者：Intelligent people. Again, Laozi is turning compliments on their heads; he referred to devious people and fakers and phony people.

第四章 和光同尘
dì sì zhāng hé guāng tóng chén

道冲，而用之或不盈。
dào chōng ér yòng zhī huò bù yíng

渊兮，似万物之宗。
yuān xī sì wàn wù zhī zōng

挫其锐，解其纷，和其光，
cuò qí ruì jiě qí fēn hé qí guāng

同其尘。
tóng qí chén

湛兮，似或存。
zhàn xī sì huò cún

吾不知谁之子，象帝之先。
wú bù zhī shuí zhī zǐ xiàng dì zhī xiān

Chapter 4. Harmony of Light and Dust

The Dao is void, but its use never exhausts.

A deep (watery) void, seems origin of all things.

Dulling its sharp edges, untangling its chaos, harmonizing its lights and merging into its dust.

Like a vast water, it just seems to always exist. I do not know who birthed the Dao, (whoever did so must have) preceded all emperors' (history).

Notes:

Previously, in Chapter 3, the author merely hinted on the conflicts due to conformity, standardization and top down interference. Now, with Chapter 4, the author explicitly started his Water theme and conflict avoidance theme, indirectly.

冲，渊，湛， are all water related. Water theme is one of the main threads of *Dao De Jing*.

The last sentences also raised the issue of Dao's origin and the author admitted the limitation of his own knowledge. Even as a preeminent historian, the author Laozi retained a refreshing humility and frankness. To be continued.

挫： dulling, obstructing
锐： sharp blade
解： solve, resolve
纷： chaos, tangles, conflicts
挫其锐，解其纷： de-escalation and resolution of conflicts
或： sometimes, often, always
象帝： apparently emperor

第五章 天地不仁
dì wǔ zhāng tiān dì bù rén

天地不仁，以万物为刍狗。
tiān dì bù rén　　　yǐ wàn wù wéi chú gǒu

圣人不仁，以百姓为刍狗。
shèng rén bù rén　　yǐ bǎi xìng wéi chú gǒu

天地之间，其犹橐籥乎？虚
tiān dì zhī jiān　　qí yóu tuó yuè hū　　xū

而不屈，动而愈出。
ér bù qū　　dòng ér yù chū

多言数穷，不如守中。
duō yán shù qióng　　bù rú shǒu zhōng

Chapter 5. Heaven's Neutrality

Heaven and Earth are not motivated by preferential Beneficence(仁), (they) consider all things, equals.
The Sage is not motivated by preferential Beneficence, (he) considers all people, equals.
Between the Heaven and Earth, lies the lung.
(It) seems empty, yet it is never exhausted; it functions by moving, breathing in and out.
Too much talking exhausts breathing, it is not as good as staying **neutral** (中).

Notes:

The opposite of preferential Beneficence（仁），"中"，center is dynamic balance, is also a sort of neutrality. In later chapters, the author will keep coming back to illustrate the neutrality principle for the Sage.

The author seemed to doubt that there were benevolent deities, nor that benevolence is a worthy leadership quality. Instead of Benevolence, neutrality and No-Interference, are the ultimate guarantees from the top.

These words would have landed him in big trouble anywhere else in ancient world, like Socrates in Athens. Socrates would have appreciated his tolerant audience in Ancient China.

This chapter ended by introducing the theme of sustainability, (the opposite of exhaustion) hand in hand, with neutrality(中). Extremes are un-sustainable, whereas, neutrality is sustainable.

刍狗：Straw dogs that are thrown away after sacrifice, hence equals.
橐籥：lungs
屈，穷：exhausting, exhausted, unsustainable.

第六章 谷神不死

谷神不死，是谓玄牝。

玄牝之门，是谓天地根。

绵绵若存；用之不勤。

Chapter 6. The Mother is Eternal

The spirit of valley is eternal, it is called the Profound Mother(玄牝).

The Profound Mother's gate, is called the root of Heaven and Earth.

Soft and tender, (it) seems to exist; (we) could use its resources but should not exhaust it.

Notes:

Legend says that Laozi was born as an old man, so he presumably witnessed his own birth. This short chapter might have been the source of these legends.

Laozi paid tribute to motherhood and use it to explain an ancient Chinese strain of environmental conservation. Eventually Laozi built up his theme of the Mother, a tender love and hope that transform into true Courage.

Historians in ancient China worked in families and clans. Its traditions and professional ethics were passed down generations. A few notable women worked as historians in ancient China especially during Daoist dynasties. It was possible that Laozi himself had horned his craft under his mother's tutelage. Later, Confucians monopolized most literary career and barred the career door to women and Daoist scholars.

The "valley" is an important theme in *Dao De Jing*, Laozi returned to it again and again. It associated with humility, plentiful, harvests, resources. This chapter deals with resource conservation.

谷：humility, plentiful, harvests, resources.
玄牝：black female beast, profound mother
勤：busy, apparently busy, busywork not complimentary.

第七章 成其私
dì qī zhāng chéng qí sī

天长地久。
tiān cháng dì jiǔ

天地所以能长且久者，以其不
tiān dì suǒ yǐ néng cháng qiě jiǔ zhě yǐ qí bù

自生，故能长生。
zì shēng gù néng cháng shēng

是以圣人后其身而身先；外其
shì yǐ shèng rén hòu qí shēn ér shēn xiān wài qí

身而身存。
shēn ér shēn cún

非以其无私邪！ 故能成其
fēi yǐ qí wú sī yé gù néng chéng qí

私。
sī

Chapter 7. Sustainable Self-Preservation

Heaven is sustainable, Earth is enduring.

Why so? Because they do not have ego, so, they are sustainable and enduring.
Therefore, the Sage will put his own body after others, thus, he will be the first of people;
(he) will go outside his own body's perspective, and thus he will preserve his own body.
It is not due to his own lack of selfish motives! Thus, he will sustain his own self-preservation.

Notes:

A true Daoist protects himself, but without self-consciousness and excessive selfishness. The author acknowledged the importance of both self-interest and group interest.

The push and shove of self-interest and group interests was a classic ideological conflict. As an historian, the author had studied, perhaps even witnessed, dynastic turmoil and collapses, resulting from excesses by both ideological camps.

Extremes on both sides of self-interest vs group interest are unsustainable. Those who believed in "outlawing private property", often caused "tragedy of commons" problems, resulting in collapse. Those who believed in the absolute selfish interest before public good, also cause collapse via widened income divide.

To avoid the dual extreme causes of social collapse, the author advocated balance and continued previous chapters' sustainability theme. A good solution, must first be a sustainable solution.

自生：ego, self-motivation, selfishness, self-interest, self-generation, self-growth. Laozi point out the difference between living systems (motivated by self-preservation, with ego) vs a system (without motivation, without ego) here.
长生：endurance, sustainability
私：self
邪：耶 exclamation

第八章 上善若水

shàng shàn ruò shuǐ
上善若水。

shuǐ shàn lì wàn wù ér bù zhēng
水善利万物而不争；

chǔ zhòng rén zhī suǒ wù   gù jǐ yú dào
处众人之所恶，故几于道。

jū shàn dì   xīn shàn yuān   yǔ shàn rén
居善地，心善渊，与善仁，

yán shàn xìn   zhèng shàn zhì   shì shàn néng
言善信，政善治，事善能，

dòng shàn shí
动善时。

fū wéi bù zhēng   gù wú yóu
夫唯不争，故无尤。

Chapter 8. Sustainable like Water

Be highly sustainable like Water.

Water benefits all things without Rivalry;

It is taken for granted by all, thus, it is likened to the Dao.
It molds itself skillfully to the place, its heart skillfully protects itself in the deep, it skillfully gives Beneficence, it speaks with credibility, it skillfully governs, it serves within capacity, it moves with perfect timing.

By offering No-Rivalry, it gets no complaint (hence it is more sustainable).

Notes:

Water and managing water were ancient China's greatest accomplishment and sources of wisdom. Its first dynasty was founded by a water engineer (Yu). Later dynasties retained a deep stake in water engineering. Water theme and No-Rivalry (conflict avoidance) theme come together in this chapter. Both will reappear throughout the book.

To Laozi, water represented the solution to the internal frictions and conflicts that often brought down empires.

"No-Rivalry", when addressed to ruling class (as Laozi seemed to be), connotes anti-monopoly policy stance.

不争：no compete, no friction, no Rivalry. This is a big theme throughout Laozi. A form of conflict avoidance and confliction resolution.
善：modern usage is translated as "kindness". But in *Dao De Jing*, this character often means sustainably skillful.
尤：blames, complaints

第九章 莫之能守

持而盈之，不如其已；
揣而锐之，不可长保。
金玉满堂，莫之能守；
富贵而骄，自遗其咎。
功遂身退，天之道。

Chapter 9. Resource Curse

Holding a vessel and filling it to the brim, it is not as good as to know when to stop.
Tempering a blade and sharpening it, (one) still could not protect (himself) forever.
Gold and jade fill a house, no one could defend it (forever).
He who is wealthy and noble, therefore proud; he himself causes his own destruction.
Better that, as soon as his mission is complete, he retires with his body intact, thus dictates Heaven's Dao.

Notes:

Elaboration of Chapter 2.
Daoist value system tended to differ from most other religions' value system. It believes that promotion of unsustainable standards, or unsustainable values, cause distortion and over time lead to unsustainability. Even worse, resources (gold, jade, wealth, power, nobility, pride) are curses, hence modern economists called them "Resource Curse". They are unsustainable and un-defendable. As a modern example, Singapore and Congo both became independent during 1960s, similar in income levels. Singapore is resource poor and Congo is resource rich. After half a century, their fortunes diverged wildly. Congo became mired in civil war waged from within and without. While Singapore enjoyed stable prosperity.

The solution for the Resource Curse? Cultivate values that is sustainable and defendable, such as love of self and body. Character, social trust and knowledge enriches future generations, while accumulation of weapons and wealth bring disasters to succeeding generations.

Body theme in the last sentence linked to Chapter 7. To be continued in Chapter 13.

盈：fill up
揣：tempering a blade
咎：blame, cause own destruction
遂：complete

第十章 载营魄抱一
dì shí zhāng zǎi yíng pò bào yī

载营魄抱一，能无离乎？
zǎi yíng pò bào yī   néng wú lí hū

专气致柔，能婴儿乎？
zhuān qì zhì róu   néng yīng ér hū

涤除玄览，能无疵乎？
dí chú xuán lǎn   néng wú cī hū

爱民治国，能无知乎？
ài mín zhì guó   néng wú zhī hū

天门开阖，能为雌乎？
tiān mén kāi hé   néng wéi cí hū

明白四达，能无为乎？
míng bái sì dá   néng wú wéi hū

生之畜之，生而不有，为而不
shēng zhī chù zhī   shēng ér bù yǒu   wéi ér bù

恃，长而不宰，是谓玄德。
shì   zhǎng ér bù zǎi   shì wèi xuán dé

Chapter 10. (Prayers) One Inside and Out

May (we) be One inside and out?

May (we) focus gently as a baby?

May (we) be cleansed as a spotless mirror?

May (we) love our people and govern our State, without treachery?

The Heaven's gate opens and closes, may it be observed calmly?

May (we) connect to clarity in all four directions, with no (distracting) interference?

It births us and nurtures us, without (claims of) ownership, cares for us without self-promotion, promotes our growth without lording over us, it is called the Profound De.

Notes:

This chapter offered a summary prayer. Laozi wrote beautiful prose-poetry, in doing so, he might have started yet another distinctive Daoist tradition.

A long lineage of Chinese poets followed, booming in the Daoist Tang Dynasty, and became extinct when Daoism lost its way subsequently. From Zhuangzi (庄子), Sima Qian (司马迁) to Qu Yuan (屈原), to Tao Yuan-Ming (陶渊明), Chen Zi-Ang (陈子昂), Li Bai(李白).

This chapter touches on several distinct characteristics of Daoism.
1) worship of philosophical concepts (道，德)
2) individualism (载营魄抱一，能无离乎)
3) pragmatic patriotism (爱民治国，无知，无为)
4) the heritage of hero philosopher, king philosopher, poet philosopher, scientist and engineering philosopher (无知，载营魄抱一)
5) simplicity (无知，无为), neutrality of history （涤除玄览，能无疵乎）, sustainability
6) respect for the weak and gender equality (能婴儿乎？能为雌乎？). Female stands for the humble, nurturing, the quietly observant. Baby stands for the neutral, the sustainable and hopes of future.

载：holding up   营魄：soul
涤除：washes off   览：mirror, history, reviews, truth   疵：spots, blemish
阖：close the door
能为雌乎: could it be observed like the females, or quietly observant?

第十一章 无之为用

Chapter 11. Powers of Without

三十辐，共一毂，当其无，有车之用。

Thirty spokes sharing a hub, **without** something, it is made useful as a cart wheel.

埏埴以为器，当其无，有器之用。

Clay is made into a vessel, **without** something, it is made useful as a vessel.

凿户牖以为室，当其无，有室之用。

Drill walls to make doors and windows of a house, **without** something, it is made habitable.

故有之以为利，无之以为用。

Therefore, **with** something (we) derive profit, **without** something (we) derive usefulness.

Notes:

Laozi expanded his theme "**with**" and "**without**" from Chapter 1 and Chapter 2.

Since "**with**" and "**without**" are equal. Value judgements and standardization based on exclusive "**with**", are doomed to failure. Laozi predicted the failures of lope-sided value systems. Instead of the obvious the-more-the-better values, like wealth, power, morality, beauty, etc., he would advocate less obvious values, such as simplicity, equality, neutrality and sustainability.

The first analogy, touches on wheel-wright's craft. Wheelwrights were like the ancient aircraft engineers, and they practiced their craft even in the presence of kings. Recent discoveries of large chariot wheels surviving from that era, featured around 30 spokes.

While raw material is still sold by weight, processing and crafts requires design of spaces. Solid wheels mostly do not perform as well as light wheels, in terms of suspension, endurance and being steerable. Solid clay mostly does not perform as containers. Solid house mostly does not offer shelter. Solid wood blocks do not perform as well as empty boats.

Through choices of "**with**" and "**without**", commodities become craft.
Through choices of "**with**" and "**without**", craft becomes art.

第十二章　为腹不为目
dì shí èr zhāng　wéi fù bù wéi mù

五色令人目盲；
wǔ sè lìng rén mù máng

五音令人耳聋；
wǔ yīn lìng rén ěr lóng

五味令人口爽；
wǔ wèi lìng rén kǒu shuǎng

驰骋畋猎，令人心发狂；
chí chěng tián liè　lìng rén xīn fā kuáng

难得之货，令人行妨。
nán dé zhī huò　lìng rén xíng fǎng

是以圣人为腹不为目。故去
shì yǐ shèng rén wéi fù bù wéi mù　gù qù

彼取此。
bǐ qǔ cǐ

Chapter 12. No Parties for the Philosopher

Five colors blind their eyes;

Five sounds deafen their ears;

Five flavors numb their taste-buds;

Riding and hunting, madden their hearts;

Rare goods tempt them astray.

Therefore, the Sage appeals to the belly, but not to the eyes. Therefore, (he) rejects that and prefers this.

Notes:

The author in one swoop, disclaimed a whole bunch of enjoyments, they are all related to **with**, as opposed to **without**. These enjoyments distort senses, and they distort reality of **without**. This chapter emphasizes "为腹不为目", preference for truth and simplicity, rejection of superficial splendor, are pragmatic leadership choice. Because the author addresses leaders throughout the book, his suggestion is counter-intuitive to most people. Yet readers of history will recognize countless leaders who lived in reality bubbles and ended in disastrous failures, before Laozi and since. I will just list three otherwise outstanding leaders who lead to particular disasters from Chinese history.

	Colors, painting, women	Music and dancing	Nice Food	Riding, hunting and war	Rare goods	Consequences
商纣王	women	X	X	X	ivory chopsticks	Revolt, nation failed and death
唐玄宗	women	X	lychee		X	Revolt, nation almost failed and declined
宋徽宗	Women and a talented painter himself.				X	Revolt, nation failed, captivity

Legend said that the author was a guest at a custom house while writing this book. He had to turn down feasts and parties; or maybe he was not invited and had sour grapes. More on feasts and parties later in Chapter 20.

腹：stomach, implies reality, basics, simple basic needs, high priority needs.
目：eyes, implies distraction, superficial splendor, passions, fantasy, low priority luxuries.
彼：that
此：this

第十三章 贵以身为天下
dì shí sān zhāng guì yǐ shēn wéi tiān xià

宠辱若惊，贵大患若身。
chǒng rǔ ruò jīng guì dà huàn ruò shēn

何谓宠辱若惊？
hé wèi chǒng rǔ ruò jīng

宠为下，得之若惊，失之若惊，是谓宠辱若惊。
chǒng wéi xià dé zhī ruò jīng shī zhī ruò jīng shì wèi chǒng rǔ ruò jīng

何谓贵大患若身？
hé wèi guì dà huàn ruò shēn

吾所以有大患者，为吾有身，及吾无身，吾有何患！
wú suǒ yǐ yǒu dà huàn zhě wéi wú yǒu shēn jí wú wú shēn wú yǒu hé huàn

故贵以身为天下，若可寄天下；
gù guì yǐ shēn wéi tiān xià ruò kě jì tiān xià

爱以身为天下，若可托天下。
ài yǐ shēn wéi tiān xià ruò kě tuō tiān xià

Chapter 13. Self-Reliance, Self-Preservation

Love and criticism both cause trauma, therefore the leader strives to preserve his Body.

So why do (I) say: "love and criticism both cause trauma"?

People who depend on love are humble, with love (they are) overly joyful, without love (or criticism, they are) overly despondent, therefore, "love and criticism both cause trauma".

Why do (I) say: "the leader strives to preserve his Body"?

My greatest danger comes from losing my Body; If I do not have the Body, then I have no danger!

Thus, if I preserve my Body from danger, then, I might be responsible for all under Heaven;

only if I love all under Heaven as I love my Body, then I could be a guardian of all.

Notes:

This chapter contrasts against Chapter 12 and 8, 7. Where Laozi previously emphasized lack of ego and ulterior motives, simplicity in life, now he emphasized importance of self. This chapter also connects to Chapter 12 and 7 and 9, in that the Sage will seek to self-preservation and preservation of his people, his team and independence by extension.

It divides into 2 sections,
1) about the dangers of external dependencies and external incentives （宠辱）
2) about the importance of self-preservation and by extension, preservation of a leader's team and independence. (贵大患若身)

This chapter is also basis for Daoist medicine. Several chapters are deeply humanist and treasures the Body more than all external rewards. Daoist medicine was greatly advanced during Daoist dynasties, Eastern Jin, Tang Dynasty. The government by respecting Daoist practice, promoted science and medicine. During these periods, Daoist scientists developed high efficient public health practices, such as antiseptic treatment of water, separation of drinking source from fecal pollution, surgeries and medicines that proved highly effective against parasitic infections such as malaria, and other killer diseases. In one anecdote, Tang dynasty Daoist Emperor Gao-Zong（唐高宗）suffered from headaches, overriding his Empress, he chose to undergo head surgery and was cured.

身：Body, core, independence

第十四章 无象之象

dì shí sì zhāng　wú xiàng zhī xiàng

shì zhī bù jiàn　míng yuē yí
视之不见，名曰夷；

tīng zhī bù wén　míng yuē xī
听之不闻，名曰希；

tuán zhī bù dé　míng yuē wēi
抟之不得，名曰微。

cǐ sān zhě bù kě zhì jié　gù hún ér wéi
此三者不可致诘，故混而为

yī　qí shàng bù jiǎo　qí xià bù mèi
一。其上不皦，其下不昧。

shéng shéng bù kě míng　fù guī yú wú wù
绳绳不可名，复归于无物。

shì wèi wú zhuàng zhī zhuàng　wú wù zhī xiàng
是谓无状之状，无物之象，

shì wèi huǎng hū
是谓恍惚。

yíng zhī bù jiàn qí shǒu　suí zhī bù jiàn qí
迎之不见其首，随之不见其

hòu
后。

zhí gǔ zhī dào　yǐ yù jīn zhī yǒu
执古之道，以御今之有。

néng zhī gǔ shǐ　shì wèi dào jì
能知古始，是谓道纪。

Chapter 14. Mysteries of Histories

Looking without seeing, call it Invisible;

Listening, without hearing, call it Inaudible;

Reaching out without attaining, call it Intangible.

These three things could not be distinguished, so together they are the One.
The One's upper (beginning) was mysterious, its lower (end) was somewhat clear.
The rope history could not be named, so it returned to Nothing.
This is called the shape of no shape, the appearance of nothing, it is called the Murk.

Facing it coming at (me), yet (I) do not see its head;
Following it from behind (me), yet (I) do not see its tail.
By holding on the ancients' Dao, (we) could govern today.

Starting from knowing the ancients' beginnings, is the Dao's Epoch.

Notes:
Up to "绳绳不可名", rope histories, this chapter seems like mysticism. Then the author made it clear that previous mysticism refers all to history of ancients, which is invisible, inaudible and intangible. Quite murky and shapeless. Following chapters seem to deal with history through the eyes of an historian. Dao De Jing is a cryptic methodology written by an ancient historian, with historians/rulers/scholars as his intended audience. The author inherited several hundred years' worth of extensive data from his forebears, which inspired its unique language.
Recent archaeological discoveries (Ma-wang-dui texts A B) cast doubt on the last two sentences. "By adapting to Today's Dao, we could govern Today", was an alternative version. It also makes sense.
This version have for 2000 years been studied by most Chinese Daoist, thus retained. Laozi might have intentionally avoided the "today" of his time. He was a historian, though he might have performed duties in contemporary record keeping, he maintained a professional reticence. As a result, Dao De Jing was unique even by ancient Chinese standard, with no references to names, places, dates. By avoiding these references, and keeping the texts simple, it became both universal and timeless.
Rising out of a rich recorded history, Daoism was half science, half philosophy and half religion, making up for a unique heritage. *Dao De Jing* laid foundation for many dynastic Constitutions/legal codes in ancient China, shed light on some of the most vexing problems, from ancient times to even today, both in China and in the USA.
恍惚：Murk, vaguely mysterious,

第十五章 古之善为道者

古之善为道者，微妙玄通，

深不可识。

夫唯不可识，故强为之容：

豫兮若冬涉川；

犹兮若畏四邻；

俨兮其若容；

涣兮若冰之将释；

敦兮其若朴；

旷兮其若谷；

混兮其若浊。

孰能浊以静之徐清？

孰能安以久动之徐生？

保此道者不欲盈。

夫唯不盈，故能蔽而新成。

Chapter 15. Ode to the Ancient Historians

Ancients who understood the Dao, they were subtle, beautiful, profound, and connected, so much so that they are incomprehensible.
Because they are so incomprehensible, let me try my best to describe their appearances:

hesitant as if crossing a river in winter;

wary as if fearful of their four neighbors;

shy like a guest;

distracted like the ice about to melt;

simple as a block;

open like a valley;

murky like muddy water.

Who could quietly let muddy water sit and cleanse itself?
Who could quietly let turmoil wear itself out to bring back Life?
As a guardian of Dao, he does not overflow (with pride).
By not overflowing with pride, he could correct old mistakes and create the new.

Notes:

The historian postdocs quietly worked to fix old mistakes and create the new. This chapter pays tribute to either to ancient rulers, lawmakers or to ancient historians. （弊而新成）Mistakes and error correction theme also echoes in Chapter 64 and subsequently.
Humility, readiness to admit errors and correction, commitment to truth, these are distinctly Daoist values.
By contrast, authorities ascribing to Confucian/Ritualists values, would be much more obsessed with appearance of infallibility. Hence, the qualities of Confucian dynasty historians suffered from their obsession.

Therefore, I name this chapter as Ode to the Ancient Historians, 史学千老之歌。

俨兮其若容： 容 may be substituted with 客，meaning guest.

第十六章 吾以观其复

致虚极，守静笃。

万物并作，吾以观复。

夫物芸芸，各复归根。

归根曰静，静曰复命。

复命曰常，知常曰明。

不知常，妄作凶。

知常容，容乃公，公乃全，全乃天，天乃道，道乃久。没身不殆。

Chapter 16. | Observe History's Cycles

To attain the ultimate emptiness, (I) faithfully maintain Stillness.
Ten thousand things grow together, I use (the Stillness) to observe their cycles.
All the living things, they return to their roots.

Returning to roots is called Stillness, the Stillness is called Cycle of Life.
Cycle of Life is called the Eternal, knowing the Eternal is called Insight.
Not knowing the Eternal, people falsely do violence.
(People by) knowing the Eternal, becomes tolerant, tolerance leads to fairness, fairness becomes complete, complete becomes heavenly, heavenly becomes Dao, Dao becomes endurance. Throughout their lives, (Dao) keep them safe.

Notes:

This chapter continues the Ode to Ancient Historians. Now it emphasizes cycles of history. Cycles are not obvious. The Confucians/Ritualists, for example, think history is progressive or linear, or of great inertia, even static: Rich and powerful people today will be rich and powerful tomorrow. Parents will always be parents, bosses will always be bosses, emperors will always be emperors, etc...

But the author said otherwise. Cycles were recognized even 2500 years ago, and most of Dao De Jing's conclusions were based on cycles. The key to observing cycles, and to know the Eternal, to gain insights into history, is to retain humility, resist bias, resist extremes, and resist linear inertia.

虚：emptiness, humility, learning altitude

静：stillness, lowkey, lack of bias, lack of volatility, moderation

笃：faithfully

妄：false, lying, wrong

凶：omen, violence, extremes

常：eternal, sustainable, constantly

不殆：nonstop

第十七章 我自然
dì shí qī zhāng wǒ zì rán

太上，不知有之；
tài shàng　　bù zhī yǒu zhī

其次，亲而誉之；
qí cì　　qīn ér yù zhī

其次，畏之；
qí cì　　wèi zhī

其次，侮之。
qí cì　　wǔ zhī

信不足焉，有不信焉。
xìn bù zú yān　　yǒu bù xìn yān

悠兮其贵言，功成事遂，百
yōu xī qí guì yán　　gōng chéng shì suì　　bǎi

姓皆谓："我自然"。
xìng jiē wèi　　wǒ zì rán

Chapter 17.   "I Follow My Own Nature"

The best (leader) is inconspicuous;

the next best (leader) is loved and praised;

the next best (leader) is feared;

the worst kind (of leader) is despised.

When Truth is lacking, there is Distrust.

The best leaders are calm and with few words, they complete their missions, and people all say: "I follow my own Nature"

Notes:

This chapter offers a test of leadership. Being a contrarian, Laozi believed that the less conspicuous leadership is also more effective; honesty and trust building are fundamental to society building. Following ones' own nature, respect for free-will, honesty are all important themes throughout *Dao De Jing*.

With this emphasis in individual freedom and honesty, the Daoists distinguished themselves throughout history in China from other schools and other religions. Daoist legal thinking underpinned all China's golden ages (Early Han Dynasty, Tang Dynasty, Eastern Jin Dynasty).

Many Daoist concepts, such as individual freedom, limits to government powers, separation of government (later chapters), were way ahead of their time. Laozi independently derived the same concepts as the American Constitution 2000 years later.

自然：Nature, free will in this context

第十八章 大道废
dì shí bā zhāng dà dào fèi

大道废，有仁义；
dà dào fèi   yǒu rén yì

智慧出，有大伪；
zhì huì chū   yǒu dà wěi

六亲不和，有孝慈；
liù qīn bù hé   yǒu xiào cí

国家昏乱，有忠臣。
guó jiā hūn luàn   yǒu zhōng chén

Chapter 18. When the Great Dao is Lost

When the great Dao is lost, people will fake Beneficence and Virtue;
When cleverness is widespread, there will be great Fakery;
When six relatives are infighting, (all six) will fake filial and parental Love;
When a State falls into misinformation and chaos, ministers will fake loyalty.

Notes:

Dao is lost by advocating lofty standards, by enforcing conformity, by faking, by distortion, by misinformation, by increases in complexity, inflexibility and infighting, difficulty in scaling.

This chapter seemed to have Confucian thinking in mind, their emphasis on Beneficence, virtue, cleverness, filial/parental love, rituals, etiquettes, emphasis on patriotic loyalty to authorities.

Some Confucian scholars claimed, that these oblique references in *Dao De Jing* to Confucian slogans meant that Laozi was later than Confucius, and his book *Dao De Jing* was also later than Confucian Classics.
There were many evidences to refute such claims:
1) Confucius was not the first ancient thinker to advocate for Beneficence, Virtue, Cleverness, Filial Duty, Loyalty, Rituals, Etiquettes. In fact, some or all of values were widely circulated for almost a thousand years before Confucius made them basis for his school of thought.
2) Most Confucian classics (original works supposedly bearing Confucius' original thinking) were not written down until after Confucius death
3) Around the same time as Confucian classics were written down, many Daoist schools were already referring to *Dao De Jing* by its author. Some important states already started to practice Daoist philosophies in their lawmaking, during the Warring States period.
4) During the Warring States period, there were many anecdotes of younger Confucius making a pilgrimage to Zhou's capital, explicitly to learn at the feet of much older Laozi.
5) Archaeologists in 20th century dug up *Dao De Jing* dated significantly earlier than Confucian classics. Based on probability, Dao De Jing should have been widely circulated and very influential while Confucian classics were being formulated.

In conclusion, *Dao De Jing* was likely a best seller, generations earlier than Confucian classics.

dì shí jiǔ zhāng jué shèng qì zhì
第十九章 绝圣弃智

jué shèng qì zhì mín lì bǎi bèi
绝圣弃智，民利百倍；

jué rén qì yì mín fù xiào cí
绝仁弃义，民复孝慈；

jué qiǎo qì lì dào zéi wú yǒu
绝巧弃利，盗贼无有。

cǐ sān zhě yǐ wéi wén bù zú gù lìng
此三者，以为文不足，故令

yǒu suǒ shǔ
有所属：

jiàn sù bào pǔ shǎo sī guǎ yù jué xué
见素抱朴，少思寡欲，绝学

wú yōu
无忧。

Chapter 19. Less Complexity

Leave out the saintly and abandon the clever, people benefit a hundred times;
Leave out the Beneficent and abandon the Virtuous, people return to filial and parental Love;
Leave out the contrivances and abandon the profitable, robbers and thieves disappear.
These three value systems (圣智，仁义，巧利) are never satisfied with enough ornaments, so (the Sage) should put them in their place: (instead he) is plain and embraces Simplicity, (he) abandons strategies and lacks ulterior motives, (he) never mimicries, therefore, (he) never worries.

Notes:

A historian got tired of watching too much faking and mimicry, too many rituals and contrivances, too many slogans and morality advocates.

Laozi continued his veiled reference to Confucians or Ritualists' main slogans. Instead, he advocated Simplicity and originality, individualism and free speech.

圣：virtuous and saintly
智：clever, crafty and treacherous
仁：beneficent and compassionate
义：righteous, justice
文：adornment
学：learning, traditionally complimentary; but *Dao De Jing*, reverses it, refer to mimicry, faking, accumulation of complexity and errors.
素，朴：Plain and Simple

第二十章 独异于人
dì èr shí zhāng dú yì yú rén

唯之与阿，相去几何？
wéi zhī yǔ ā xiāng qù jǐ hé

善之与恶，相去若何？
shàn zhī yǔ è xiāng qù ruò hé

人之所畏，不可不畏。
rén zhī suǒ wèi bù kě bú wèi

荒兮，其未央哉！
huāng xī qí wèi yāng zāi

众人熙熙，如享太牢，如春登台。
zhòng rén xī xī rú xiǎng tài láo rú chūn dēng tái

我独泊兮，其未兆，如婴儿之未孩；儡儡兮，若无所归。
wǒ dú bó xī qí wèi zhào rú yīng ér zhī wèi hái lěi lěi xī ruò wú suǒ guī

众人皆有余，而我独若遗。
zhòng rén jiē yǒu yú ér wǒ dú ruò yí

我愚人之心也哉，沌沌兮！
wǒ yú rén zhī xīn yě zāi dùn dùn xī

俗人昭昭，我独昏昏。
sú rén zhāo zhāo wǒ dú hūn hūn

俗人察察，我独闷闷。
sú rén chá chá wǒ dú mèn mèn

澹兮其若海；飂兮若无止。
dàn xī qí ruò hǎi liù xī ruò wú zhǐ

众人皆有以，而我独顽似鄙。
zhòng rén jiē yǒu yǐ ér wǒ dú wán sì bǐ

我独异于人，而贵食母。
wǒ dú yì yú rén ér guì shí mǔ

Chapter 20. Different from Others

Approval vs disapproval, how much difference is there?
Goodness vs evil, how much difference is there?
What people fear, must (*not-not/double negative*) be fear worthy.
There is a vast endless desert (of possibilities)!
Joyful crowds appear to hold a ceremonial feast, parading up a vantage point in spring.

I alone am detached, looking for un-seeable omens, (crying alarm) like a pre-language baby. Lonely am I, as if I am without a home.

The crowds all seem to enjoy surplus, only I seem to have nothing left.
My foolish heart, murky!
The ordinary people are clear, I alone am foggy.
The ordinary people are prying, I alone am indifferent.

Like the lights playing on ocean waves;
Like the gusts blowing on and on.
The crowds all seem similar, only I seem different and lowly.
I am different from others, because (History's Dao) is my precious Mother's Milk.

Notes:

This historian seemed to have had a Cassandra moment. His contemporaries failed to understand why he feared so-and-so, like the Saintly, the Clever, the Loving, the Righteous, the Contrivances and the Profitable.
He must have been a sore thumb, the rain on parades, the ancient wall flower at their happy parties and their happy rituals. He did not see what others see. His methods, his inspiration, and his motivation all came from a different time and a different place.
Like Cassandra, he predicted correctly, but was mostly unheeded. His lonely voice of reason was for thousand years, drowned out by flowery slogans, false sense of security, shiny fancy and moral orthodoxy.

第二十一章 惟道是从

孔德之容，惟道是从。

道之为物，惟恍惟惚。

惚兮恍兮，其中有象；

恍兮惚兮，其中有物。

窈兮冥兮，其中有精；

其精甚真，其中有信。

自古及今，其名不去，以阅众甫。

吾何以知众甫之然哉。

以此。

Chapter 21. Only Follow the Dao

The great De appears to only follow the Dao.

Dao's manifestation, is only murky.

Murkily, inside are signs;

murkily, inside are contents.

Profoundly interesting, inside is Essence;
Essence is very True, inside it, there is Information.

From antiquity to today, its Name is eternal, in it we observe the Father of all.

How do I know to find the Father of all?

Based on these signs...

Notes:

De 德 is elaborated here and will take on more weight further on.

While Dao is the algorithm of universe, the scientific principles that underlie the complex systems;
De refers to human heuristics, with the goal of adapting to Dao, the heuristics that help make better choices.

名：Name, title, History's Truth.
甫：Father

第二十二章 曲则全

曲则全，枉则直，洼则盈，
敝则新，少则得，多则惑。
是以圣人抱一为天下式。

不自见，故明；

不自是，故彰；

不自伐，故有功；

不自矜，故长。

夫唯不争，故天下莫能与之
争。

古之所谓曲则全者，岂虚言
哉！

诚全而归之。

Chapter 22. Flexibility is Preserved

The flexible is preserved, the bent is straightened, the low spot became water laden, the worn-out is renewed, the few gets more, the multitude is distracted.
Therefore, the Sage will embrace the One to become role model for all.

He does not show-off, therefore, he is clear;
he does not consider himself all-correct, therefore, he is corrected;
he does not brag, therefore, he is successful;

he is not proud, therefore, he is sustainable.

Due to his lack of rivalry, no one could rival him.

Ancient historians wrote: "The Flexible is preserved", they did not make it up!

They honestly preserved Flexibility and kept its ways.

Notes:

No-Rivalry, Humility, Flexibility are themes of De, these are personal heuristics to live by, sustainably.

第二十三章 信不足焉

希言自然。

故飘风不终朝，骤雨不终日。

孰为此者？天地。

天地尚不能久，而况于人乎。

故从事于道者，同于道；

德者，同于德；

失者，同于失。

同于道者，道亦乐得之；

同于德者，德亦乐得之；

同于失者，失亦乐失之。

信不足焉，有不信焉。

Chapter 23. When Truth is Lacking

Less talk is natural.

Therefore, gusts do not last the whole morning, storms do not last the whole day.

Who made these? Heaven and Earth.
If Heaven and Earth could not (keep up violence) for a long time, how could people (keep up violence for a long time)?
Therefore, people who follow Dao, they share the same (path of) Dao;
people who follow De, they share the same (path of) De;
people who follows neither, they go their separate ways.
Sharing the (path of) Dao, Dao will bring them Joy.
Sharing the (path of) De, De will bring them Joy.
Sharing the (path of) Neither, neither will bring them Joy.
When Truth is lacking, there is Distrust.

Notes:

This is the second time, *Dao De Jing* mentions "When Truth is lacking, there is Distrust" (previously in Chapter 17). Much slogan is just a symptom, violence is just a symptom, "Truth is lacking", is the real cause.

Laozi pointed out hopefully that "violence is unsustainable", he offered a glimmer of hope that people will return to honest peace. This optimistic line sustained people in difficult times and circumstances,.

The author also makes a curious suggestion, the path of Dao, De and neither, should split, in order to bring peace. He also repeats this suggestion later.

This chapter illustrates the author's own unstable times; the author also offered diagnosis (lack of Trust); and spoke of Hope for survivors.

第二十四章 余食赘形

企者不立；

跨者不行；

自见者不明；

自是者不彰；

自伐者无功；

自矜者不长。

其在道也，曰余食赘形。

物或恶之，故有道者不处。

Chapter 24. Extra Food and Burden

Standing on tiptoes is unstable;

big strides are unsustainable;

people, who show off, will lose clarity into Truth;

people, who think themselves correct, they will not be corrected;

boastful people will lose their boasts;

prideful people will not endure.
These (faults) are like the extra food and cancerous burden to the Dao.
These (faults) turn things into adversaries, therefore, people with Dao will avoid such.

Notes:

More expansion of Chapter 22.

Laozi repeatedly advocated for self-truth, history-truth, self-knowledge, sustainability Simplicity and trust. Laozi rejected forms of contrivances and extraneous complexity.

Complex systems are less sustainable, complex strategies are less workable, complex projects are less scalable.

赘: extra

第二十五章 周行而不殆

有物混成，先天地生。

寂兮寥兮，独立而不改，周行而不殆，可以为天下母。

吾不知其名，字之曰道，强为之名曰大。

大曰逝，逝曰远，远曰反。

故道大，天大，地大，人亦大。

域中有四大，而人居其一焉。

人法地，地法天，天法道，道法自然。

Chapter 25. History's Big Cycles

Something was mixed up, formed before the Heaven and Earth.

Quietly by itself, independent and unchangeable, it endlessly cycles, to become the Mother of All.

I do not know its name, I call it Dao. If I have to describe it, I will call it the Big.

So big that it disappears into Infinity, so disappeared that it is far away. So far away, it returns to its origin point.
Therefore, Dao is Big, Heaven is Big, Earth is Big, Human* is also Big.

The Universe has Four Big (Cyclical players), and Human* is one of the Four.

Humans follow the (cyclical) Laws of the Earth,
The Earth follow the (cyclical) Laws of Heaven,
Heaven follows the (cyclical) Laws of Dao,
Dao follows the (cyclical) Laws of Nature.

Notes:

This chapter starts with universe genesis hypothesis, then moves on to a hypothesis of a long-term cycles involving astronomical bodies, earth and human society, ruled by the implicit yet universal and unchangeable Dao. The author again clarified that there was a boundary to contemporary human knowledge, and that he named Dao out of conceptual necessity, rather than theological or moral certainty. "I do not know its name", "I call it the Big" "I call it Dao", hence, "大道" (the Big Dao).

* Human (人居其一) in some version is "King" (王居其一). But this does not fit with subsequent context, when context switched back to Human (人法地).

Then the author clarified the big cyclical Players of universe and exalt human's status as one of the Big Players. Finally, the author laid out the Order of Laws, that Human -> Earth -> Heaven -> Dao -> Nature.
The author as a custodian of History, should be well versed in Astronomy, Geology and Hydrology as well. Modern readers should keep this in mind.

法: laws, principles, following the cycles of nature

第二十六章 重为轻根

重为轻根，静为躁君。

是以君子终日行不离辎重。

虽有荣观，燕处超然。

奈何万乘之主，而以身轻天下？

轻则失根，躁则失君。

Chapter 26. Heavy Anchors the Reckless

Heavy anchors the reckless, Stillness rules the impatient.
Therefore, a ruler retains his burden all day even in his far-flung travels.
Though he appears brilliant, he remains detached.
Why should the ruler of ten thousand chariots behave recklessly towards his own Body and his State?

The reckless will lose their roots, the impatient will lose their control.

Notes:

Laozi seemed to address an audience. Who? We do not know but venture several reasonable guesses:

1) Legends have it that a provincial custom officer was his main audience: he probably have asked questions about promotions, famous personalities, taxes, border defense, gods and spirits, harvests, resource management, emergency management, immigration,etc..

2) Legends also stated that Laozi was a chief historian employed by the Zhou emperor, or at least a King of a major state. Hence, "万乘之主" a ruler of ten thousand chariots is addressed in this chapter。

3) As a Zhou dynasty historian, Laozi might have taught Kings and Emperors and assorted princelings. They would be interested in leadership, historic figures, histories, taxes, border defense, gods and spirits, harvests, resource management, emergency management, immigration management.

This chapter seemed to be addressing heads of state directly. The more prosperous and populous a State, the more its center of gravity (and control) will move out of the (nominal) leaders. This is inevitable. Laozi advised detachment and Stillness, to keep the center of gravity within, thus to avoid toppling.

The more prudent and still, you must be. Says Yoda-Laozi.

Soon, Laozi will address questions about other important topics of ancient statecraft, such as the army and military force.

dì èr shí qī zhāng　cháng shàn jiù rén
第二十七章 常善救人

shàn xíng wú zhé jì　　shàn yán wú xiá zhé
善行无辙迹，善言无瑕谪，
shàn shù bú yòng chóu cè
善数不用筹策；
shàn bì wú guān jiàn ér bù kě kāi　　shàn jié
善闭无关楗而不可开，善结
wú shéng yuē ér bù kě jiě
无绳约而不可解。
shì yǐ shèng rén cháng shàn jiù rén　　gù wú qì
是以圣人常善救人，故无弃
rén
人。
cháng shàn jiù wù　　gù wú qì wù　　shì wèi
常善救物，故无弃物，是谓
xí míng
袭明。
gù shàn rén zhě　　bù shàn rén zhī shī
故善人者，不善人之师；
bù shàn rén zhě　　shàn rén zhī zī
不善人者，善人之资。
bù guì qí shī　　bù ài qí zī
不贵其师，不爱其资，
suī zhì dà mí　　shì wèi yào miào
虽智大迷，是谓要妙。

Chapter 27. Sustainable Savior

A master walker leaves no tracks, a master speaker stays blameless, a master accountant requires no counting-aids;

a master craftsman makes a seamless lock box that is impossible to break in, a master knot maker makes that unsolvable knot without obvious knots.

Similarly, the Sage saves people sustainably, hence leaves no one behind.

(He) seeks to conserve resources, hence leaves no trash, such is called "inheriting Clarity (of Dao)".

Therefore, the masters are teachers to the noobs;
while the noobs provide for the masters.
(People who) do not respect the masters, who do not cherish the noobs,
though they may be crafty, they are quite lost, such (mutual respect) is considered necessary Wisdom.

Notes:

Laozi in this chapter paid tribute to the crafts and wisdoms of all lineages. Daoism later evolved to become a unique Chinese philosophy-religion, producing bumper crops of scientists, doctors, engineers, historians, poets and politicians in ancient China.

袭明：Inheriting clarity. This contrasts with Chapter 52.

第二十八章 复归于朴

知其雄，守其雌，为天下溪。

为天下溪，常德不离，复归于婴儿。

知其白，守其黑，为天下式。

为天下式，常德不忒，复归于无极。

知其荣，守其辱，为天下谷。

为天下谷，常德乃足，复归于朴。

朴散则为器，圣人用之，则为官长。

故大智不割。

Chapter 28. Return to Plain and Simple

Knowing the male, retaining the female, (Dao) is the creek of the world.

(With Dao) being the creek of the world, constant Virtue (*De*) means to stay with (Dao), returning to a baby's naiveté.
Knowing the white, retaining the black, (Dao) is the model of the world.
(With Dao) being the model of the world, constant Virtue (*De*) does not depart, but returns to Neutral (pole-less).

Knowing the glory, retaining the humility, (Dao) is the valley of the world.

(With Dao) being the valley of the world, constant Virtue (*De*) is plenty, returning to the Plain and Simple.
The Plain and Simple is usable as a vessel, the Sage uses (the Plain and Simple) to fulfill his office.

Therefore, the greatest Wisdom does not cut or injure.

Notes:

De (Virtue) appears occasionally before Chapter 10, 21, 22. De is increasing weight from this chapter on.

朴：Plain and Simple
德：Virtue means following the Dao. By definition, it's different from most Confucian virtues.
式：Model
守： retain, protect,
无极：Pole-less, center, middle, neutral, Murk

第二十九章 为者败之

将欲取天下而为之，吾见其不得已。

天下神器，不可为也，不可执也。

为者败之，执者失之。

故物或行或随；

或嘘或吹；

或强或羸；

或载或隳。

是以圣人去甚，去奢，去泰。

Chapter 29. Controlling it will Destroy it

He who wants to take over the world and control it, I think he will not succeed.

The world is a sacred vessel, one could neither control it, nor hold onto it.

Controlling it will destroy it, holding onto it, will lose it.
Therefore, all things may be self-driven or followers;
may inspire or expire;

may be strong or weak;

may be stable or falling apart.

Therefore, the Sage avoids excesses, avoids extravagance, avoids conceit.

Notes:

Remember the author had a Cassandra moment, when his Truth was not appreciated by the audience. This is one of the unfortunate chapters bearing bad forecast for ambitious leaders of the free world (in ancient China).

More to follow in Chapter 30.

Similar to the US Constitution, Laozi advocated limitation to government powers.

载：stable, holding up
隳：lazy, falling apart
去：avoid, remove

第三十章 物壮则老

以道佐人主者，不以兵强天下，其事好还。

师之所处，荆棘生焉；

大军之后，必有凶年。

善者果而已，不敢以取强。

果而勿矜，果而勿伐，果而勿骄。

果而不得已，果而勿强。

物壮则老，是谓不道，不道早已。

Chapter 30. Unsustainable Violence

The ruler who follows the Dao, would not use his soldiers to intimidate the world, then his efforts get better returns.

Wherever an army pass through, thorns spring up;
A great military mobilization always omens a disastrous year.

A sustainable ruler merely sets his goals, daring not to preempt with violence.
(He) achieves goal without pride, (he) achieves goal without boasting, (he) achieves goal without conceit.
(He) achieves goal only because of necessity, (he) achieves goal (preferably) without use of violence.
Things, (especially armies), grow strong then decline into old age, so call it "without Dao", "without Dao" will soon pass out.

Notes:

This chapter delivers more bad news for the elite audience. Their prided armies are problematic. For many reasons, but ultimately, this chapter touches on the least obvious causes: unsustainability of violence.

Sustainability is one of the unique insights of *Dao De Jing*.

凶年： a disastrous year. After the great armies sweep through, there would be poor harvests, famines, epidemics.

第三十一章 胜而不美

dì sān shí yī zhāng shèng ér bù měi

夫佳兵者，不祥之器，物或
fū jiā bīng zhě　bù xiáng zhī qì　wù huò

恶之，故有道者不处。
è zhī　gù yǒu dào zhě bù chù

君子居则贵左，用兵则贵
jūn zǐ jū zé guì zuǒ　yòngbīng zé guì

右。
yòu

兵者不祥之器，非君子之
bīng zhě bù xiáng zhī qì　fēi jūn zǐ zhī

器。不得已而用之，恬淡为
qì　bù dé yǐ ér yòng zhī　tián dàn wéi

上。
shàng

胜而不美，而美之者，是乐
shèng ér bù měi　ér měi zhī zhě　shì lè

杀人。
shā rén

夫乐杀人者，则不可得志于
fū lè shā rén zhě　zé bù kě dé zhì yú

天下矣。
tiān xià yǐ

吉事尚左，凶事尚右。
jí shì shàng zuǒ　xiōng shì shàng yòu

偏将军居左，上将军居右，
piān jiàng jūn jū zuǒ　shàng jiāng jūn jū yòu

言以丧礼处之。
yán yǐ sāng lǐ chù zhī

杀人之众，以悲哀泣之；
shā rén zhī zhòng　yǐ bēi āi qì zhī

战胜，以丧礼处之。
zhàn shèng　yǐ sāng lǐ chù zhī

Chapter 31. Military Metrics are Body-Counts

The best military force is still not an auspicious vessel. (It turns) things into adversaries, therefore a ruler of Dao should avoid using (military force).
The civilian ministers occupy the prized left-hand side, while the military staff occupies the right-hand side.

Military force is not an auspicious vessel, therefore, (it) is not civilian staff's preferred vessel. Out of necessity he uses the military, though he is indifferent (to military gain therefore he is) above (violence).

(Civilian ministers) will not glorify victory, since people who glorify victory, are glorifying body-counts.

Such people who glorify body-counts, would not receive honors under Heaven.

In auspicious celebrations, the left-hand side is honored, in funerals, the right-hand side is honored.
Lower ranked military officers occupy the left, the top ranked military officers occupy the right, as in funeral processions.

The more body-counts, the more mourning; victory in war, is greeted with funeral mourning.

Notes:

The author continued to expound his almost pacifist views. His reasons are outlined as follows: in addition to unsustainability, military policies and organizations also observe a radically different agenda and metrics (body counts), rather than their civilian counter parts. So Laozi advocate the separation of these two organizations, as well as emphasis of civilian leadership, sustainable and humanist metrics, civilian control over military leadership; again, Laozi's conclusions were remarkably modern and similar to the American Constitution 2000+ years later.
This chapter also resolves a vexing problem in many societies, how military vs civilian staff should be ranked according to protocol. The two branches have opposite metrics, hence are ranked on the opposite sides independently.

第三十二章 莫之令而自均

道常无名。

朴虽小*，天下莫能臣也。

侯王若能守之，万物将自宾。

天地相合，以降甘露，民莫之令而自均。

始制有名，名亦既有，夫亦将知止，知止可以不殆。

譬道之在天下，犹川谷之于江海。

Chapter 32. Of Their Own Free-Will

Dao Eternally goes by No-Title.

(Dao is) plain and small, yet nothing under heaven could subjugate it.
If princes could follow Dao, then all things, of their own free-will, will come to be (their) guests.

Heaven and Earth complement each other to make sweet rain. People could not order (the rain to fall), yet of their own free-will share (it).

First Rules are made, then Titles are given. When there are (enough) Titles, time to call a stop; (princes should) also know when to stop, thus to allow sustainable continuation (of these Rules).
The Dao is to the world, (their destiny), like creeks running to rivers, then to the sea.

Notes:

Rain in ancient China was a sacred symbol of Heaven's Grace, and by extension the Emperor or King's favor.

This chapter speaks of a fundamental resource allocation problem. Inequity and non-transparency in Rules, lack of adherence to Rules, have plagued many a Chinese dynasty; many dynasties were still-born or collapsed early due to injudicious allocation of Titles and resources. Allocation problem remains fundamental to modern societies.

This chapter is similar to the US Constitution. It elevates Rules and prefers the simple, the plain, and the small over complexity. The individual free-will is the basis for the group's will.

名：Names, Titles
宾：guest, client, officers, subjects
朴虽小*： is in some version, not in other version
自均：self-share, self-equalize, evokes a randomization process "return to norm", as in Chapter 77.

第三十三章 自知者明

知人者智；自知者明。

胜人者有力；自胜者强。

知足者富；强行者有志。

不失其所者久，死而不亡者

寿。

Chapter 33. Know Themselves

Those who know others, has craft; those who know Themselves have Clarity.
Those who triumph over others, is forceful; those who triumph over Self are strong.
Those, who content themselves, are wealthy; those who triumph over adversity have will.
People who do not lose themselves, could endure; those who die but are not forgotten, they have longevity.

Notes:

Dao De Jing advocates individualism. Self-knowledge was high on the author's list of virtues.

This chapter also accepts Death yet opens up the possibility of eternal remembrance beyond death. This is a traditional Chinese concept. Longevity and remembrance, Immortality are all big themes in Daoism. Also, see Chapter 54.

第三十四章 大道不辞

大道泛兮，其可左右。

万物恃之以生而不辞；功成不名有。

衣养万物而不为主，常无欲，可名于小。

万物归焉而不为主，可名为大。

以其终不自为大，故能成其大。

Chapter 34. Great Dao Takes Responsibility

The Great Dao is vast, its choices go left and right.
All things depend on Dao to survive, yet Dao does not shirk its responsibility; when his mission is complete then he retires to obscurity.

Dao clothes and nurtures all things without enslaving them, without ulterior motives, and gets small recognitions.

All things return to Dao, but Dao does not claim control, therefore Dao is called great.

Because the Dao does not think itself great, therefore it becomes the Great Dao.

Notes:

Ancient Daoists participated in politics but through their own peculiar political tradition (distinct from Confucian tradition). They did their duties then retired into obscurity. They saved their people then left glory behind. 范蠡，张良，谢安 might have recognized George Washington as fellows.

There were six typically Daoist lay-professional undertakings. Many tended to be polymaths spanning multiple careers. Following table shows typical career choices:

	Hermits	Politicians, Economists	Scientists Historians Engineers Doctors	Poets Painters Artists	Soldiers Swordsmen Military leaders	Merchants
范蠡	X	X				X
张良	X	X				
谢安	X	X		X	X	
李白	X			X	X	
范仲淹		X		X	X	
张仲景，孙思邈，李淳风，祖冲之等	X		X	X		

泛: boating on a vast water body

第三十五章 往而无害

执大象，天下往。

往而不害，安平泰。

乐与饵，过客止。

道之出口，淡乎其无味；

视之不足见；

听之不足闻；

用之不足既。

Chapter 35. Approach without Harm

Whoever holding the great model (Dao), all under Heaven will want to approach (him).
(All could) approach without harm, and all find peace, stability and security.
Music and food, passers-by stop to savor.

Yet, Dao tastes to the mouth, plain without flavor;

(we) look at it, without seeing (Dao);

(we) listen to it, without hearing (Dao);

(we) use it, without exhausting (Dao).

Notes:

In this chapter, Laozi offered advices regarding immigration and recruiting policy. At the time, there were many competing states in the mini-UN called China.

A state that follows Dao, attracts talent without fanfare and keeps them.

A good recruiting policy, does not harm, it does not tempt, it does not ensnare, it does not deceive.

第三十六章 弱胜强

将欲歙之，必故张之。

将欲弱之，必故强之。

将欲废之，必故兴之。

将欲取之，必故与之。

是谓微明。

柔弱胜刚强。

鱼不可脱于渊，国之利器不可以示人。

Chapter 36. The Flexible Prevails

Intent to collapse it, first make it expand.

Intent to weaken it, first make it forceful.

Intent to lay it waste, first make it powerful.

Intent to take over it, first give it something.

This is the obscure clarity of (Dao).

The flexible weak prevails over the inflexible powerful.
Fish could not liberate itself from the river, a nation's sharp instruments should not be brandished about.

Notes:

This chapter is continuation of previous chapter 35. No threats, no brags. Hubris before the fall. The weak, the flexible, the low-key shall prevail.

Its fundamental insight is of system science. Negative feedback systems are more stable (将欲弱之，必固强之) than positive feedback systems (which is liable to exponential growth, flameouts, and collapse, vicious cycle, etc.). To be continued in Chapter 40,58, 81. Tai-chi（太极）and 5-Xing（五行）diagrams are fundamentally system diagrams.

This chapter embodies many principles of Tai-chi martial arts and military arts.

歙： draw in, restrain
张： expand
取： take
与： give
利器：sharp tools, symbolizing power, advantage, projections of power

第三十七章 天下将自定

dì sān shí qī zhāng tiān xià jiāng zì dìng

dào cháng wú wéi ér wú bù wéi
道常无为而无不为。

hóu wáng ruò néng shǒu zhī　　wàn wù jiāng zì
侯王若能守之，万物将自

huà
化。

huà ér yù zuò　　　wú jiāng zhèn zhī yǐ wú míng
化而欲作，吾将镇之以无名

zhī pǔ
之朴。

wú míng zhī pǔ　　　fū yì jiāng bù yù
无名之朴，夫亦将不欲。

bù yù yǐ jìng　　　tiān xià jiāng zì dìng
不欲以静；天下将自定。

Chapter 37. Self-Regulate for Balance

Dao mostly avoids Interference, but it (*double negative*) gets things done.

If rulers could keep to it, all things will self-regulate.
Even in self-regulation, still there will be destructive competition, I would suppress destructive competition with (Dao), through "Simplicity that goes by No-Name".
Through "the Simplicity that goes by No-Name", self-regulation will avoid the pitfalls of destructive competition.
By showing no bias and suppressing destructive competition, I prefer Stillness; all things under Heaven will self-adjust to reach balance.

Notes:

Bias, is the beginning of the end. Bias introduces systemic errors and persist them. *Dao De Jing* is about reaching equilibrium with Self and through Self. The ultimate goal is a peace, equilibrium, balance to self-love, self-respect, self-regulate, self-control, self-educate, self-adjust.

欲 in this context, is interpreted the unbounded ambition, competitive behavior that obstructs cooperation, that over time lead to destructive competition. In any self-regulated complex system, whether economics or politics or cultural, destructive competition is a powerful undercurrent, sometimes overwhelmingly the main current. Unchecked, the system will likely suffer violent turmoil.

为： interference, act, act of service, service
无为： No-Interference, No (Apparent) Action, no grandstanding, no faking
无不为： full of action
无欲： no bias, no ulterior motives, lack of ambition
自化： self-educate, self-regulate
自定： self-adjust to reach equilibrium, keep calm and carry on.

第三十八章 上德不德

上德不德，是以有德。

下德不失德，是以无德。

上德无为而无以为；

下德为之而有以为。

上仁为之而无以为；

上义为之而有以为。

上礼为之而莫之应，则攘臂
而扔之。

故失道而后德，失德而后
仁，失仁而后义，失义而后
礼。

夫礼者，忠信之薄，而乱之
首。

前识者，道之华，而愚之
始。

是以大丈夫处其厚，不居其
薄；处其实，不居其华。

故去彼取此。

Chapter 38. Being Contrarian is a Virtue

The highest Virtue (*De*) lacks consciousness of Virtue, therefore it is Virtuous.

The lowest Virtue (*De*) holds on to an (artificial) Virtue, therefore it is not Virtuous.

The highest Virtue (*De*) does No-Interference, and does not presume (Interference is good).

The lowest Virtue (*De*) advocates Interference, and it presumes (Interference is good).

The highest Beneficence advocates Beneficence and does not presume (Beneficence is good).*

The highest Justice advocates Justice and presumes (Justice is good). *

The highest Ritualist advocates Rituals and when nobody cares for Rituals, he would force Rituals on people.

Therefore, failing Dao, fallback is to use Virtue (*De*). Failing Virtue (*De*), the next fallback is Beneficence. Failing Beneficence, the next fallback is Justice. Failing Justice, the next fallback is Rituals.

Rituals, are flimsy substitutes for loyalty and trust, their (contrived) prevalence herald chaos.

People who think ahead, they got the Dao's essence, becoming a (contrarian) Fool.

Therefore, a great man stands on the thick (Dao), avoids the flimsy (Rituals); he stands on the solid ground, and avoids flowery adornments.

Therefore, (he) avoids that (flowery rituals) and prefers this (contrarian Dao).

Notes:

A little background: Ritualists advocated Rituals as a universal cure for all ailments. Ritualist is also another name for Confucianism, because Confucius specialized in rituals, etiquettes and orthodoxy. Their scholarship focused on the rituals, pomp, orthodox morality and etiquettes of the increasingly irrelevant Zhou Federal Government.   Confucians solution to social ills included moral slogans, appearances, legal enforcement of orthodoxy and rituals.

In this chapter, the author criticized the Ritualist tendency to force uniform appearances (orthodoxy) on people, distorting genuine information, enforcing artificial uniformity, silencing dissenters.   These activities masked real systemic problems, built up distrust, were difficult to scale up, even heralded cultural/government collapse.

The author was contrarian, as he repeatedly claiming himself as foolish. (愚)

*: there were two lines that may have been errors introduced in the subsequent 2000 years of Confucian total-dominance, or they could be honest mix-ups.

shàng rén wéi zhī ér wú yǐ wéi
上仁为之而无以为；

shàng yì wéi zhī ér yǒu yǐ wéi
上义为之而有以为。

第三十九章 珞珞如石

昔之得一者：

天得一以清，地得一以宁，神
得一以灵，谷得一以生，侯王
得一以为天下正。

其致之：天无以清，将恐裂；

地无以宁，将恐废；

神无以灵，将恐歇；

谷无以盈，将恐竭；

万物无以生，将恐灭；

侯王无以贵高，将恐蹶。

故贵以贱为本，高以下为基。

是以侯王自谓孤、寡、不
谷，此非以贱为本邪！非乎？

故致数誉无誉。

是故不欲琭琭如玉，珞珞如
石。

Chapter 39. Prefer being a Rock

Ancients got the One:

Heaven got the One to become clear, the Earth got the One to become peaceful, spirits got the One to become divine, valleys got the One to become plentiful (of life), princes got the One to steer the country in the right (direction).

Here's why: the Heaven without (the One's) clarity, should fear collapse;

the Earth without (the One's) peace, should fear waste;

the spirits without (the One's) divinity, should fear lost;

the valleys without (the One's) plenty, should fear exhaustion;

all things without (the One's) life force, should fear extinction;

princes without (the One)'s nobility, should fear being toppled.

Therefore, the noblemen has commoner base, the elevated has basement.

Similarly, princes refer to themselves as the "orphaned", the "widowed", the "un-plenty", is that not (describing) their base station! Is that not so?

Truly, multitudes of honors are like none at all. Therefore, (sage leaders) would rather not be like precious jades, but rather be like the common rocks.

Notes:

Once again, Laozi advocated a unique (far ahead of its time) value system. He preferred rock over jade. He preferred the "base" over the "elevated". The One is better than the multitudes. Less is more. Simple is beautiful. Truth comes from dissenters. Contrarians make better decisions. Violence is unsustainable. Strength is weakness. Opposites are useful endpoints.

第四十章 有生于无

反者道之动。

弱者道之用。

天下万物生于有，有生于无。

Chapter 40. Feedback Loop

The existence of contraries gives Dao its dynamic power.
The existence of weak gives Dao its applicability (to protect and nurture).

All things under Heaven are born **with** (Dao),
With (Dao) are born from **without** (Dao).

Notes:

This chapter first emphasizes contrary and weak. Then it echoes back to the Chapter 1: **with** and **without**.
This chapter describes a dynamic feedback loop. The weak and powerful, the dissents and assents are all nodes in a system. They are equal, so Dao flows through all the nodes, from 0 to 1, then from 1 to 0, and everywhere in between.

Chapter 43, Chapter 64, Chapter 78, elaborate this chapter.

第四十一章 闻道测试

dì sì shí yī zhāng wén dào cè shì

shàng shì wén dào, qín ér xíng zhī
上士闻道，勤而行之；

zhōng shì wén dào, ruò cún ruò wáng
中士闻道，若存若亡；

xià shì wén dào, dà xiào zhī
下士闻道，大笑之。

bù xiào bù zú yǐ wéi dào
不笑不足以为道。

gù jiàn yán yǒu zhī
故建言有之：

míng dào ruò mèi, jìn dào ruò tuì, yí
明道若昧，进道若退，夷

dào ruò lèi
道若纇；

shàng dé ruò gǔ, dà bái ruò rǔ
上德若谷，大白若辱；

guǎng dé ruò bù zú, jiàn dé ruò tōu
广德若不足，建德若偷；

zhì zhēn ruò yú, dà fāng wú yú
质真若渝，大方无隅；

dà qì wǎn chéng, dà yīn xī shēng, dà
大器晚成，大音希声，大

xiàng wú xíng
象无形。

dào yǐn wú míng
道隐无名。

fū wéi dào, shàn dài qiě chéng
夫唯道，善贷且成。

Chapter 41. Dao Tests and Dao is Tested

The upper gentleman hears the Dao, he is soon busy practicing it.
The middle gentleman hears the Dao, he seems to hear it yet not quite.
The lower gentleman hears the Dao, he laughs at it.

If a Dao is not laughed at, then Dao is not the real Dao.
Therefore, (I) propose to identify Dao thus:

Clear Dao seems obscure, progressive Dao seems regressive, flat Dao (road) seems bumpy;

The highest Dao seems like a valley, Honorable behavior seems humiliating;
The broadest Virtue seems not enough, constructive Virtue seems like lazy (not interfering);
True Nature seems to waver, a big square has no corners;
A big vessel is slow in forming, a big melody has no voice, and a big view has no shape.

Dao obscures itself behind No-Name.

But only Dao, masterfully lends out and accomplishes constructively.

Notes:

The first three sentences contain two tests.
1) The gentlemen are tested according to their sensitivity and receptiveness to the Dao.
2) The Dao is also tested by the lower gentlemen's response, which is the key response.

Dao is distinguished by not resorting to fear, not hurling threats, not faking nor tempting to fake. Only if the lower gentleman feels safe enough to laugh at Dao, middle gentleman feels safe enough to appear to ignore it (think it through), upper gentlemen feels safe enough to practice it, then it is the true Dao. This is a key test for Dao.

Then the author continued to expound on the signs of invisible Dao. His words foreshadowed Adam Smith's "invisible hands of Economics" 2000+ years later.
The signs were distinctly contrarian. The author found appearances deceptive, and he preferred looking under hood.

第四十二章 损之而益
dì sì shí èr zhāng sǔn zhī ér yì

道生一，一生二，二生三，
dào shēng yī yì shēng èr èr shēng sān

三生万物。
sān shēng wàn wù

万物负阴而抱阳，冲气以为
wàn wù fù yīn ér bào yáng chōng qì yǐ wéi

和。
hé

人之所恶，唯孤、寡、不
rén zhī suǒ è wéi gū guǎ bù

谷，而王公以为称。
gǔ ér wáng gōng yǐ wéi chēng

故物或损之而益，或益之而
gù wù huò sǔn zhī ér yì huò yì zhī ér

损。
sǔn

人之所教，我亦教之。
rén zhī suǒ jiào wǒ yì jiào zhī

强梁者不得其死，吾将以为
qiáng liáng zhě bù dé qí sǐ wú jiāng yǐ wéi

教父。
jiào fù

Chapter 42. Less Is More

Dao birthed the One, the One birthed the Two, the Two birthed the Three, and the Three birthed ten thousand things.

(These) ten thousand things are backed by the Yin, to embrace the Yang. These two Forces (Chi) yield (to each other) to Balance.

Normal people, of all things, abhor being "orphaned", being "widowed", and "lacking in plenty". Yet princes refer to themselves as such (abhorrence).

Therefore, with things, less is more, or, more is less.

What others teach, I also teach the same.

Forceful robbers do not get it therefore they lose their lives, this is the core of my teaching.

Notes:

Key message is: less is more, more is less. This chapter illustrates Laozi's Razor, a scientific principle that ancient China found then almost forgot.

Being contrarian, independent and creative, paves the path to Simplicity, Balance, Harmony.

The positions of Yin and Yang are worth noting. The weaker Yin is at the back, being protected from Yang, also forming a trustworthy wall to lean to, and seeds to grow in future to come. Yang is being faced squarely, yet in an embrace.

The opposite position protecting the strong Yang while facing the weaker Yin, is not mentioned. Unlike the familiar Yin-Yang diagram (later formulation), in *Dao De Jing*, Yin and Yang are not symmetrical.

Forceful robbers could be reference for tyrants from the highest echelon. Also see Chapter 53.

和：balance, harmony and peace
气：Chi, forces, energy
损：reduce to less, deprive, less
益：increase, benefits, more

第四十三章 不言之教
dì sì shí sān zhāng bù yán zhī jiào

天下之至柔，驰骋天下之至
tiān xià zhī zhì róu　　chí chěng tiān xià zhī zhì

坚。
jiān

无有入无间，吾是以知无为
wú yǒu rù wú jiàn　　wú shì yǐ zhī wú wéi

之有益。
zhī yǒu yì

不言之教，无为之益，天下
bù yán zhī jiào　　wú wéi zhī yì　　tiān xià

希及之。
xī jí zhī

Chapter 43. Teachings of No-Talk

The most flexible under Heaven, vanquishes the toughest under Heaven.

Without and **with** enter into intimate embrace, hence I understand the benefits of No-Interference.

The teachings of No-Talk, the benefits of No-Interference, nothing under Heaven could match (them).

Notes:

The author in the last couple lines of Chapter 42, 43, turned to teaching methods.

Laozi did not seem to devote his life to teach or to persuade. Occasionally when the author did speak up, he was pithy, yet peerless. He passed down his lessons in history, and in doing so, laid down principles of critical thinking and scientific inquiry. He was a role model that inspired generations of Chinese historians and scientists, politicians and poets, merchants and soldiers, common folks.

第四十四章 知止不殆
dì sì shí sì zhāng zhī zhǐ bù dài

名与身孰亲？
míng yǔ shēn shú qīn

身与货孰多？
shēn yǔ huò shú duō

得与亡孰病？
dé yǔ wáng shú bìng

甚爱必大费；
shèn ài bì dà fèi

多藏必厚亡。
duō cáng bì hòu wáng

知足不辱。 知止不殆。
zhī zú bù rǔ   zhī zhǐ bù dài

可以长久。
kě yǐ cháng jiǔ

Chapter 44. Knowing When to Sell

Fame or body, which is dearer?

Body or goods, which is more?

Gains or losses, which is more problematic?

Strong attachment will entail much expense.

Too much wealth will entail a rich burial.

If (someone) knows when to be content, then (he) will not be humiliated. If (someone) knows when to stop, then (he) will not be entrapped. Therefore, (he) will sustain and endure.

Notes:

Author ventured now into an advice column for the leader as an investor. Leaders must consider many investment decisions, whether in people, locations, or in industries or in branches of government. There are decision biases, which often trapped the unwary. Laozi advised his audience to know when to stop, to sell, to disengage, to disperse, to be content.

Dao De Jing, published sometime 2500 years ago, gave birth to many schools of thoughts in ancient China; its short pithy messages, formed foundation for engineering and medical sciences, historic sciences, military, political, business and economics.

孰： which, who
病： sick and problematic
藏： collecting, owning
厚： rich and abundant

第四十五章 清静为天下正

dà chéng ruò quē qí yòng bù bì
大成若缺，其用不弊。

dà yíng ruò chōng qí yòng bù qióng
大盈若冲，其用不穷。

dà zhí ruò qū dà qiǎo ruò zhuō dà biàn
大直若屈，大巧若拙，大辩

ruò nè
若讷。

jìng shèng zào hán shèng rè
静胜躁*，寒胜热*。

qīng jìng wéi tiān xià zhèng
清静为天下正。

Chapter 45. Stillness-Clarity Rights the World

The great achievement seems lacking, its uses have no drawbacks.
The great fulfillment seems to be empty, yet its uses are infinite.
The great straightness seems to flex, the great craft seems to be clumsy, and the great debate seems stuttering.

The Stillness overcomes the impatient.* The coolness overcomes the hot. *
(With) Stillness and Clarity, we could right the world.

Notes:

The author was pragmatic, not fond of debates. If he was the principal of a school, the grading system for this school would be rather different from Ritualists. This chapter first echoes Chapter 41.

Then in the last two sentences, he also seemed to speak to a ruler on legislative matters. Stillness and Clarity, implies following legislative principles:

1) 清： transparency, simplicity, cool clarity. This is the opposite of 热：which means hot and turbulent.
2) 静： slow consistency builds confidence. This is the opposite of 躁：impatient and mercurial, inconsistent

These principles are very important in designing constitutions. The American Constitution follows many of the same principles as Laozi.

* The traditional text seemed to have had a mix-up here. I translate the best as I could, based on context. "躁胜寒*，静胜热*", straight translated as "The quick tempered overcomes the cold. * The stillness overcomes the hot. *"

I rearranged as above.

正：carry out justice, right the course

第四十六章 走马以粪

天下有道，却走马以粪。

天下无道，戎马生于郊。

祸莫大于不知足；

咎莫大于欲得。

故知足之足，常足矣。

Chapter 46. The Horse Test

When the world follows Dao, war horses end up pulling the dung-cart.
When the world fails to follow Dao, mares have to birth ponies on battlefield.
The worst disasters come from not being content;
The worst errors come from insatiable greed for more.
Therefore, (we) know when to be content, then (we) could have sustainable plenty.

Notes:

The author continued to speak to a ruler. He outlined a different test for the quality of their leadership, a unique Horse Test. Whether their leadership is sustainable in the long term, shows up in the fates of their horses. When mares are called to battlefields, the next generation will suffer.

He further warned against greed and vainglory; rulers must appreciate what they have and avoid traps of belligerence. "知足之足", knowing when to be content, means knowing the boundary, the thin red line between life and death. This will be systematically explained in Chapter 50 and beyond.

第四十七章 不行而知

不出户，知天下；

不窥牖，见天道。

其出弥远，其知弥少。

是以圣人不行而知，不见而明，不为而成。

Chapter 47. Foresight without Action

Without going out the door, (he) knows the world.
Without looking out the window, (he) sees the Heaven's Dao.
The farther (he) physically ventures out, the less (he) knows.
Therefore, the Sage foresees without action, clarifies without showing off, succeeds without apparent action.

Notes:

The author was apparently privileged with an extensive accumulation of historic knowledge, and as a historian, he was also versed in astronomical data. He seemed to refer to astronomy (不窥牖, 知天道) in this chapter.

This chapter seemed a rare personal chapter, applicable to himself plus very limited number of lucky scholars and ruling class. For most ancient people, getting out and practicing were important to understanding the world.

However, if the author is addressing rulers, he may be addressing privacy issues: that the rulers should not to pry and interfere in the private sectors; and that scholars need to avoid invading privacy of ordinary people.

行: is ambiguous. could be either action or going out.
见: show off, see, apparent

第四十八章 为道日损

为学日益，为道日损。

损之又损，以至于无为。

无为而无不为。

取天下常以无事，及其有事，不足以取天下。

Chapter 48. Practice Dao with Laozi's Razor

Mimic learning is practiced by adding Complexity daily; (in contrast,) Dao is practiced by cutting Complexity daily.
(Complexity is) cut and cut again, until there is No-Interference.
No-Interference, is the purest form of Action (*double negative*).
Leading the world is sustainable only through No-Interference. Too much Interference is not sustainable enough to lead the world.

Notes:

The author is less personal than Chapter 47. but still there is continuation of the Complexity theme. Laozi favors Simplicity; by now, it should be very clear.

Complexity is an enemy to system design. Because complexity introduce moving parts, introduce obfuscation, introduce fragility, introduce non-transparency, introduce unpredictability. Complex systems are difficult to scale. Ultimately, complex systems fail disastrously.

No mimicking, No-Interference, and simplicity are secrets to sustainable system design. Any system, or organization, legal or mechanical or economical, will benefit from Laozi's principles.

学：study is direct translation. But in *Dao De Jing*, it often seems to refer to some sort of faking and taking on increasing complexity.
无为： No Apparent Action, No Grandstanding, No faking
损： cut down the complexity
益： *Dao De Jing* sometimes use 益 positively. but in this case, it seems to refer to increasing Complexity, therefore not euphemistic.

第四十九章 圣人无常心

圣人无常心，以百姓心为心。

善者，吾善之，不善者，吾亦善之，德善。

信者，吾信之，不信者，吾亦信之，德信。

圣人在天下，歙歙，为天下浑其心，百姓皆注其耳目，圣人皆孩之。

Chapter 49. Lack of Prejudice

The Sage avoids extreme judgments, he respects the people's judgments.

People with skills, I respect them. People lacking in skills, I also respect them. Skills are (dimensions of) Virtue (*De*).

Trustworthy people, I trust them. Un-trustworthy people, I also trust them. Trust is (dimension of) Virtue (*De*).

The Sage under Heaven, he breathes in (thus taking in true information), his heart is empty and unprejudiced for all under Heaven. All people vent to him as if they are his eyes and ears, and the Sage treat them as equal children.

Notes:

This chapter continue to describe key characteristics of sustainable leadership, such as lack of prejudices, lack of presumptions, Simplicity, humility.

In America, these personal characteristics are collectively called "judicial temperament", worthy of a judge. Judicial temperament: neutral, decisive, respectful and composed.

善： often translated to kindness or goodness. But in *Dao De Jing*, this word often means a sustainable skill.

第五十章 善摄生者
dì wǔ shí zhāng shàn shè shēng zhě

出生入死。
chū shēng rù sǐ

生之徒，十有三；
shēng zhī tú shí yǒu sān

死之徒，十有三；
sǐ zhī tú shí yǒu sān

人之生，动之死地，亦十有三。
rén zhī shēng dòng zhī sǐ dì yì shí yǒu sān

夫何故？以其生生之厚。
fū hé gù yǐ qí shēng shēng zhī hòu

盖闻善摄生者：路行不遇兕虎；入军不被甲兵；
gài wén shàn shè shēng zhě lù xíng bù yù sì hǔ rù jūn bù bèi jiǎ bīng

兕无所投其角，虎无所措其爪，兵无所容其刃。
sì wú suǒ tóu qí jiǎo hǔ wú suǒ cuò qí zhǎo bīng wú suǒ róng qí rèn

夫何故？以其无死地。
fū hé gù yǐ qí wú sǐ dì

Chapter 50. Sustainable Survivors

People exit Life, to enter Death.

People positioned for Life, and lived, three out of ten;
People positioned for Death, and died, three out of ten;
People positioned for Life, yet they moved voluntarily to Death, also three out of ten.

Why is this? Because the last 3/10 people are excessively exhausting their lives.
(Finally, there are 1/10 exceptions.) I often hear of the sustainable survivor: he travels in wilderness and manages to avoid the rhinos and tigers; he enters the battlefield, yet avoids being injured by soldiers;
rhinos could not gorge him with their horns, tigers could not maul him with their paws, and soldiers could not cut into him with their blades.
Why is this? Because these 1/10 exceptional survivors avoid vulnerable positions of Death.

Notes:
Game theory time for Laozi's lucky audience.

	Positioned to Live(生地)	Positioned to Die(死地)
Live(生)	3/10 the Lucky Lottery Winners （生之徒）	**1/10 the Survivors of Anything （善摄生者，其无死地）Chapter 50,55**
Die(死)	3/10 the Profligate Losers （以其生生之厚） Chapter 53	3/10 the Unlucky Losers （死之徒）

The author first enumerated the probability of 3, 3, 3 out of 10.

Only one corner of square was missing 1/10: the Survivor who was put into position of Death, but managed to survive sustainably.

Then Laozi started to describe this 1/10 Survivors with more detail. To be continued in the following chapters 55. The less skillful 3/10 Profligate Losers (以其生生之厚者)，will also be further described later in Chapter 53. Laozi was interested in statistical outliers, the people whose strategies yielded exceptional results, for good or for worse.

第五十一章 尊道贵德

dì wǔ shí yī zhāng zūn dào guì dé

dào shēng zhī   dé chù zhī   wù xíng zhī
道生之，德畜之，物形之，
shì chéng zhī
势成之。
shì yǐ wàn wù mò bù zūn dào ér guì dé
是以万物莫不尊道而贵德。
dào zhī zūn   dé zhī guì   fū mò zhī mìng
道之尊，德之贵，夫莫之命
ér cháng zì rán
而常自然。
gù dào shēng zhī   dé chù zhī   zhǎng zhī yù
故道生之，德畜之，长之育
zhī   chéng zhī shú zhī   yǎng zhī fù zhī
之，成之熟之，养之覆之。
shēng ér bù yǒu   wéi ér bù shì   cháng ér
生而不有，为而不恃，长而
bù zǎi   shì wèi xuán dé
不宰，是谓玄德。

Chapter 51. De's Prayer

Dao births us, De (*Virtue*) nurtures us, physics shapes us, (hidden) potential energy assists us.

Therefore, ten thousand things (*double negative*) respect Dao and honor De.
Dao commands respect, De commands honor, Dao and De do not follow human commands but they always follow Nature.

Therefore Dao, births us, De (*Virtue*) nurtures us, (they) grow us and care for us, complete us and ripen us, nourish us and protect us.

(De) births us without (claims of) ownership, serves us without self-promotion, promotes our growth without lording over us, it is called the Profound De.

Notes:

This prayer's ending that is almost symmetric to Chapter 10. It emphasizes Profound De, slightly more than previous version of prayer. Because original texts were copied on bamboo sticks, tied together in sheets, so potentially mix-ups could impact chapter orders and line orders, also could introduce redundant chapters. Readers may want to keep this in mind.

Again, Dao is the universal principles and algorithm.
De is more about human understanding and adapting to Dao. De is the human heuristic software.

Dao follows Nature, De follows Dao. "自然" means free will in people, is translated as Nature when universally applied to non-anthropological context.

dì wǔ shí èr zhāng tiān xià yǒu shǐ
第五十二章 天下有始

tiān xià yǒu shǐ yǐ wéi tiān xià mǔ
天下有始，以为天下母。

jì dé qí mǔ yǐ zhī qí zǐ
既得其母，以知其子；

jì zhī qí zǐ fù shǒu qí mǔ méi qí
既知其子，复守其母，没其

bù dài
不殆。

sāi qí duì bì qí mén zhōng shēn bù
塞其兑，闭其门，终身不

qín
勤。

kāi qí duì jì qí shì zhōng shēn bù
开其兑，济其事，终身不

jiù
救。

jiàn xiǎo yuē míng shǒu róu yuē qiáng
见小曰明，守柔曰强。

yòng qí guāng fù guī qí míng wú yí shēn
用其光 ，复归其明，无遗身

yāng shì wèi xí cháng
殃，是为袭常。

Chapter 52. Dao is Mother

The world had an origin, presumably its Mother.

Once we understand the Mother, we understand the Child better;

Once we understand the Child, we could return to protect the Mother, so throughout our lives we are secured.

Stuff their mouth, close doors on them, their lives are not over-busy.

Open their mouth, keep bailing them out, their lives are not saved.

Paying attention to the little things, is called clarity. Protecting the weak and being flexible, is called strength.
To use (the Mother's) light, to re-illuminate clarity, then to avert all disasters, it is called "Inheriting the Eternal".

Notes:

Chapter 52 seems to continue Chapter 50 (systematic enumeration of life strategy outcomes). Survival of children requires increasing independence and self-knowledge. At the same time, we could understand beginnings (Mother) better, and conserve the resources. The child and mother relationship might also refer to causal relationship. This is called the sustainable Dao, core to emergency management, enterprise and environmentalism.

Laozi advocated a pragmatic value system, such that is applicable to investigate, to troubleshoot, to build up and to sustain.

While Chapter 27 earlier spoke of 袭明, this chapter speaks of 袭常.

袭：inheriting, reaching for
兑：marsh, mouth of a watery body where two waters mix up. Here it seems to mean mix-up in causal relationships.

第五十三章 民好径

dì wǔ shí sān zhāng mín hào jìng

shǐ wǒ jiè rán yǒu zhī, xíng yú dà dào,
使我介然有知，行于大道，

wéi shī shì wèi
唯施是畏。

dà dào shèn yí, ér mín hào jìng
大道甚夷，而民好径。

cháo shèn chú, tián shèn wú, cāng shèn xū
朝甚除，田甚芜，仓甚虚；

fú wén cǎi, dài lì jiàn, yàn yǐn shí
服文采，带利剑，厌饮食，

cái huò yǒu yú, shì wèi dào kuā
财货有余，是为盗夸。

fēi dào yě zāi
非道也哉！

Chapter 53. The Shortcut Test

Since I got the least common sense, I walked the Great Way (Dao), fearful of straying.

The Great Way (Dao) is very flat, but people prefers shortcuts.
Courts are extravagant, fields are deserted, granaries are empty;
(Yet princes) primp in finery, wear sharp swords, bored with food and drink. Much wealth is concentrated in them, thus they become boastful robbers.
This is very much not Dao!

Notes:

The author offers another visual test for "Not Dao". Similar to previous "Horse test" in Chapter 46. Dao is full of visual signs of unsustainability. Military violence is unsustainable, widening wealth gap is unsustainable. Sometimes the tests are negative tests, sometimes tests are positive tests.

This chapter also continues chapter 50, the enumeration of outcomes. Particularly the "Profligate Losers" square, where people who are positioned to live, yet end up in Death (死之徒).

	Positioned to Live(生地)	Positioned to Die(死地)
Live(生)	3/10 the Lucky Lottery Winners （生之徒）	1/10 the Survivors of Anything （善摄生者，其无死地）Chapter 50,55
Die(死)	**3/10 the Profligate Losers** （以其生生之厚） **Chapter 53**	3/10 the Unlucky Losers （死之徒）

朝甚除：Courts and palaces are extravagantly beautiful. (or very corrupt by some translation). But corruption is often masked by beauty. therefore, I prefer the direct translation: a physical description of the courts.

dì wǔ shí sì zhāng　xiū zhī yú shēn
第五十四章 修之于身

shàn jiàn zhě bù bá　　shàn bào zhě bù tuō
善建者不拔，善抱者不脱，
zǐ sūn yǐ jì sì bù chuò
子孙以祭祀不辍。
xiū zhī yú shēn　　qí dé nǎi zhēn
修之于身，其德乃真；
xiū zhī yú jiā　　qí dé nǎi yú
修之于家，其德乃余；
xiū zhī yú xiāng　　qí dé nǎi cháng
修之于乡，其德乃长；
xiū zhī yú guó　　qí dé nǎi fēng
修之于国，其德乃丰；
xiū zhī yú tiān xià　　qí dé nǎi pǔ
修之于天下，其德乃普。
gù yǐ shēn guān shēn　　yǐ jiā guān jiā　　yǐ
故以身观身，以家观家，以
xiāng guān xiāng　　yǐ guó guān guó　　yǐ tiān xià
乡观乡，以国观国，以天下
guān tiān xià
观天下。
wú hé yǐ zhī tiān xià rán zāi　　yǐ cǐ
吾何以知天下然哉？以此：

Chapter 54. Observe through Evidence

The masterful builders' buildings are never uprooted, the masterful martial artists' embrace is inescapable, their never-ending heirs will enshrine their mastery.

In his body's travail, Virtue (De) is tested;

In his family's travail, Virtue (De) is abundant;

In his community's travail, Virtue (De) is persisted;

In his nation's travail, Virtue (De) is plentiful.

In the world's travail, Virtue (De) is propagated. Therefore, observe a body through the body's evidence, observe a family through the family's evidence, observe a community through the community's evidence, observe a nation through the nation's evidence, observe the world through the world's evidence.

How do I know world's De is like this? Here is my evidence:

Notes:

This chapter along with Chapter 42, formed spiritual backbone for Tai Chi martial arts and Chinese architecture engineering. 祭祀 means ritual to commemorate ancestors and teachers often at specialized shrines. Ancient China was dotted with ritual shrines, dedicated to heroes, poets, politicians, doctors and engineers and craftsmen. Such shrines persisted the Chinese collective cultural memory, thus, formed the backbone of Chinese heritage. This line along with "死而不亡者寿" (Chapter 33), together informed us an ancient historian's view of immortality.

Chinese traditions often found their spiritual inspiration from *Dao De Jing*. Legendary architects and engineers, healers and herbalists, law-makers, poets, heroes, economists, craftsmen were also enshrined in the Chinese memory through Daoist literary Canons(道藏), beginning in *Dao De Jing*. These were "people of life", the immortals.

Then, this chapter expands the whole argument, and warns against overgeneralization: 以身观身，以家观家，以乡观乡，以国观国，以天下观天下。 When systems vastly differ in scale, from micro to macro, lessons drawn from smaller scale systems sometimes fail to apply to large scale systems; and vice versa. Laozi advocated applying lessons from other systems of similar scale, avoiding hasty generalization across scale factors.

天下： all under Heaven, world
祭祀： rituals, commemorating ancestors, gods, heroes, other dead that benefited the community

第五十五章 德比赤子

Chapter 55. Virtue of a Bare Baby

含德之厚，比于赤子。

毒虫不螫，猛兽不据，攫鸟不搏。

骨弱筋柔而握固。

未知牝牡之合而朘作，精之至也。

终日号而不嗄，和之至也。

知和曰常，知常曰明。

益生曰祥，心使气曰强。

物壮则老，是谓不道，不道早已。

(He who has) abundant Virtue (*De*) is comparable to a bare Baby.
Poisonous insects will not sting (him), fierce beasts will not maul (him), predatory birds will not attack (him).

(His) bones are weak, (his) sinews are flexible and (his) grasps firm.

(He) does not yet know male and female's coupling, yet his member is up and ready, showing that his internal circuit is whole.
(He) cries all day without hoarseness, showing the ultimate Balance.
Knowing Balance is called Sustainable.
Knowing Sustainable is called Clarity.
Benefiting Life is called Auspice, letting Heart command the Force (Chi) is called Strength.
Things (like all Life) grow strong then decline into old age, so call it "**without** Dao", **without Dao**, things will soon pass out.

Notes:
This chapter also is continuation of chapter 50, the enumeration of outcomes, particularly the Survivors square, describing people who escape Death into Life. Perhaps, while Laozi was staying at the guesthouse, a baby cried day and night. Then someone got angry and complained, so Laozi delivered this chapter.

The greatest survivor's trick is to be like a baby. Why so? A baby is small, yet he is a complete system, a perfect embodiment of the Daoist virtues:
1) He is true to his own self. He does not lie or pretend or flatter.
2) He is weak and flexible.
3) He is designed to be neutral (unprejudiced) and balanced.
4) He is nonthreatening, harmless and lovable.
5) He has potential.
6) He has complete internal circuits. Feedback loops that stabilize, virtuous cycles that grow.
This chapter links to Chapters 10, 20, 28, 30, and 42.
赤子： bare baby Links to Chapters 10, 20, 28.
气： Chi also gets mentioned here, like Chapter 42.
精： essence, circuit of essence.
物壮则老，谓之不道，不道早已： Last sentence repeats from Chapter 30. Strength, power and bias are the seed for destruction, superpowers are on the brink for decline, the high flier stock are good for selling. They are the opposite to the Baby.

第五十六章 知者不言

知者不言，言者不知。

塞其兑，闭其门，挫其锐，解其纷，和其光，同其尘，是谓玄同。

故不可得而亲，不可得而疏；

不可得而利，不可得而害；

不可得而贵，不可得而贱。

故为天下贵。

Chapter 56. Confidentiality and Neutrality

People who know do not talk, people who talk do not know.
Plugging their mouths, closing doors on them, dulling their sharpness, untangling their chaos, harmonizing their lights and merging into dust, this is called the Profound Empathy.

Therefore, (they are) beyond familiarity, beyond distance;
beyond profit, beyond harm;

beyond glorification, beyond humiliation.

(They) will be honored under Heaven.

Notes:

This chapter echoes Chapter 4, 52. Laozi continued to advise audience as leaders, particularly in positions that may require neutrality and confidentiality, perhaps as arbitrators or judges in disputes.

This chapter is on how to have empathy, to maintain confidentiality, to be neutral, to resolve conflicts by knowing but not talking, to be sensitive to potential conflicts of interest.

玄：Profound, this is a recurring theme in *Dao De Jing*. Chapters 1, 6, 10, and 15, 65.
玄同：Profound empathy or sameness.

第五十七章 以无事取天下
dì wǔ shí qī zhāng yǐ wú shì qǔ tiān xià

以正治国，以奇用兵，以无事取天下。
yǐ zhèng zhì guó yǐ qí yòng bīng yǐ wú shì qǔ tiān xià

吾何以知其然哉？以此：
wú hé yǐ zhī qí rán zāi yǐ cǐ

天下多忌讳，而民弥贫；
tiān xià duō jì huì ér mín mí pín

人多利器，国家滋昏；
rén duō lì qì guó jiā zī hūn

人多伎巧，奇物滋起；
rén duō jì qiǎo qí wù zī qǐ

法令滋彰，盗贼多有。
fǎ lìng zī zhāng dào zéi duō yǒu

故圣人云："我无为而民自化；我好静而民自正；我无事而民自富；我无欲而民自朴。"
gù shèng rén yún wǒ wú wéi ér mín zì huà wǒ hào jìng ér mín zì zhèng wǒ wú shì ér mín zì fù wǒ wú yù ér mín zì pǔ

Chapter 57. Unintended Consequences

(Leaders should) use Justice to rule the nation, use unexpected tactics to lead military, use No-Interference to win over the world.

How do I know it is so? Because of (unintended consequences):
The more prohibitions in the world, the poorer are its people;
the more people wield sharp weapons, the more chaos is in this nation;

the cleverer people are, the more exceptions spring up everywhere;
the more legislations are enacted and enforced, the more robbers and thieves show up.
Therefore, the Sage said: "I prefer No-Interference, so that people could self-regulate; I prefer Stillness, so that people will self-correct; I take No-Trouble, so that people will be self-sufficient; I show No-Preference, so that people will simplify themselves.

Notes:

Laozi first offered three key points of success as leaders of Free World (in ancient China). Apparently, Laozi's audience did not argue with Justice (以正治国), nor did they argue with unexpected tactics （以奇用兵）, but the audience did seem to doubt the last point: 以无事取天下， "Why is No-Interference recommended for the ultimate leadership? We do not agree…"

So, Laozi elaborated the last point, his explanation involved four examples of "unintended consequences".
And then he fully expanded his prescription of no-actions: No-Interference, Stillness, No-Trouble, No-Preference.
Ultimately the sustainable goals are for the people to self-regulate, self-correct, self-sufficient, self-simplify.

Compare with the US Constitution.

自化：echoes chapter 37.

第五十八章 福祸倚伏
dì wǔ shí bā zhāng fú huò yǐ fú

其政闷闷，其民淳淳；
qí zhèng mèn mèn qí mín chún chún

其政察察，其民缺缺。
qí zhèng chá chá qí mín quē quē

祸兮福之所倚，福兮祸之所
huò xī fú zhī suǒ yǐ fú xī huò zhī suǒ

伏。
fú

孰知其极?
shú zhī qí jí

其无正也。
qí wú zhèng yě

正复为奇，善复为妖。
zhèng fù wéi qí shàn fù wéi yāo

人之迷，其日固久。
rén zhī mí qí rì gù jiǔ

是以圣人方而不割，廉而不
shì yǐ shèng rén fāng ér bù gē lián ér bù

刿，直而不肆，光而不耀。
guì zhí ér bù sì guāng ér bù yào

Chapter 58. Fortune's Reversal

If the government are indifferent, the people are simple.
If the government are prying, the people lack (honesty).

Disasters are foundation to fortune, and fortune hide the seed of disasters.

Who knows where or when the reversal of extremes would come?
Because there may not be a resting equilibrium for cycles of fortune-disasters.
The Righteous reverses itself to become tactical. The Good reverses itself to become evil.
People are mystified (by these reversals), since ancient times.
Therefore, the Sage are square without cutting others, they have integrity without giving offense, they are straight without taking license, they give light without blinding others.

Notes:

It also echoes Chapter 20. But whereas in Chapter 20, the author writes of himself, now the author speaks more clearly of governance.
The author also seemed to warn of government invasion of privacy (其政察察).

Then it turns to one of the many famous lines: describing how disasters turn to good fortune and vice versa. The reversal of fortune is mystifying, its timing unpredictable; hence even ancients remarked them with fascination. But Laozi was in a unique position to explain it systematically. Reversal of fortunes has internal system logic:
large systems have multiple layers of cycles, therefore requires dynamic balance and feedback loops to regulate, in order to avoid falling into chaos of extremes, which is often irreversible.

This logic is fundamental to many of *Dao De Jing*'s enigmas. Complexity, too many moving parts, conformity and standardization that masks real problems, heavy promotion of moral orthodoxy, strength and violence, interference, micromanagement, reckless speeding are all unsustainable, un-scalable and lead to irreversible disasters.
Thus, this chapter also further explains previously stated (Chapter 57) No-Interference prescriptions. The Sage would avoid extreme positions, stay true yet avoid offensive self-righteousness, be honest without being abrasive.

正复为奇： continues Chapter 57 "以正治国，以奇用兵". 正 means righteousness, justice, white swans. 奇 means oddball, tactical, black swans.

第五十九章 长生久视
dì wǔ shí jiǔ zhāng   cháng shēng jiǔ shì

治人事天，莫若啬。
zhì rén shì tiān，   mò ruò sè

夫唯啬，是谓早服。
fū wéi sè，   shì wèi zǎo fú

早服谓之重积德。
zǎo fú wèi zhī zhòng jǐ dé

重积德则无不克。
zhòng jǐ dé zé wú bù kè

无不克则莫知其极；
wú bù kè zé mò zhī qí jí

莫知其极，可以有国。
mò zhī qí jí，   kě yǐ yǒu guó

有国之母，可以长久；
yǒu guó zhī mǔ，   kě yǐ cháng jiǔ

是谓深根固柢，长生久视之
shì wèi shēn gēn gù dǐ，   cháng shēng jiǔ shì zhī

道。
dào

Chapter 59. Enduring Life and Persistent Gaze

To regulate human affairs and to serve Heaven's affairs, best use a farmer's husbandry.
Only with farmer's husbandry, there could be planning ahead.
Planning ahead means accumulating Virtue (*De*).
Once enough Virtue (*De*) accumulated, anything could be accomplished (*double negative*).
Once anything could be accomplished, then (the ruler) will not have to deal with the extremes.
Without extremes, (a ruler) could govern a cohesive nation.
A cohesive nation, governed through its Mother (Dao), could endure.
Such is how (the ruler) should ensure deep and firm roots, the Dao of Enduring Life and Persistent Gaze.

Notes:

This chapter continues to advise the ruler. How should one bootstrap a sustainable nation for long term success? the same advices apply to any organization, especially at the startup and early stage:
1) Planning ahead
2) Accumulate goodwill, become self-sufficient, accumulate self-knowledge, etc.
3) Avoid extremes.

Bootstrapping and long-term Sustainability are key goals for Daoism. This chapter compares these efforts to farmers' husbandry. Though the farmer is starving, he saves up his winter seeds for next year's harvest. Then he cultivates his crops.

In my translation, I often translate 国 into "State". Historically, during Laozi's time, China was a semi-federate nation, many states were effectively ruled by their own dukes and kings with Zhou dynasty 天子's blessings (the actual blessing event usually happened a few hundred years before Laozi's own time); each state was effectively their own "nation", with its own laws, its own unique culture, its own writing and dialect; they shared common religious beliefs and language and value systems; they are honor bound to serve the same common Zhou Dynasty Federacy. Subsequently, some states became dominant to gain superpower status and finally, only one state managed to conquer all other states to form a new dynasty (Qin Dynasty), spelling the end to the Zhou Dynasty multi-state federation system. I could have translated 国 into "nation" instead, and often I do.

啬：harvest, farming, husbandry, miserly, may mean starving farmers saving up their winter seeds for future sowing.
根柢：root
视：watch, observe, gaze. Daoism is very observant and committed to truth and unbiased information

第六十章 其神不伤人

dì liù shí zhāng qí shén bù shāng rén

zhì dà guó ruò pēng xiǎo xiān
治大国若烹小鲜。

yǐ dào lì tiān xià qí guǐ bù shén
以道莅天下，其鬼不神。

fēi qí guǐ bù shén qí shén bù shāng rén
非其鬼不神，其神不伤人。

fēi qí shén bù shāng rén shèng rén yì bù shāng
非其神不伤人，圣人亦不伤

rén
人。

fū liǎng bù xiāng shāng gù dé jiāo guī yān
夫两不相伤，故德交归焉。

Chapter 60. Supernatural Test

Regulating a big State is like cooking a small fish (carefully).

When the nation is governed through Dao, the spirits will not manifest supernaturally.

Not that they do not manifest supernaturally, even if they manifest, they do not hurt people.

Not only that the spirits do not hurt people, the Sage also does not hurt people.

Because the two do not hurt each other, therefore the Virtue (De) converges.

Notes:

The first sentence was famous overseas because US President Reagan quoted it. However, what it means is not clear. Most likely it was a continuation of previous chapter, suggesting that audience should avoid extremes, avoid haste and avoid overzealous government interference.

It also evokes Chinese food. Since times immemorial, Chinese chefs and Chinese engineers ruled China. Yi Yi was once a lowly cook, but eventually became the legendary prime minister of early Shang dynasty more than 3000 years ago. His laissez-faire altitude was distinctly Chinese chef.

Laozi aside from his professional interest in history, might have enjoyed cooking and engineering and crafts. Later Daoist philosophers Zhuangzi also inherited this respect for cooks and craftsmen.

After this short first sentence (which I devoted three paragraphs to explain), Laozi moved on from cooking. To establish two tests, one for supernatural, another for leaders.

The author lived in an age, when people commonly believed in ghosts and spirits and sacrifices. Here he separated the two worlds and made a test to discriminate good spirits (with Dao) vs evil spirits.

1) Spirits with Dao: they do not hurt people. they do not threaten nor claim human sacrifice. etc.
2) Spirits without Dao: they hurt people. They threaten and destroy and claim sacrifices

The same test is used to test the Sage.

1) Sage: they do not hurt people.
2) Not Sage: they hurt people. They threaten and destroy and claim sacrifices and sow distrust.

The author concluded that the human and supernatural do not intersect in the normal course of Dao. This was not a trivial conclusion and probably had ample evidence support at the time. As this was apparently one of his audience's main concern, this audience might have been a ruler for a big state. To be continued in the next chapter.

During the Classic Chinese period, when this text was written, many scholars and rulers moved away from supernatural explanations for human affairs. That Laozi could boldly pronounce the non-intersection of two worlds, was itself nontrivial; it meant that priestly vendors of supernatural had already lost enough power and prestige. Laozi was able to spread his learning in ancient China unmolested, while ancient Greek philosopher Socrates from the same time period had to pay his life's price.

Not only the human and supernatural do not intersect to harm, leaders and their followers also do not intersect to harm.

第六十一章 各得其所欲

大国者下流，天下之交，天下之牝。

牝常以静胜牡，以静为下。

故大国以下小国，则取小国；

小国以下大国，则取大国。

故或下以取;或下而取。

大国不过欲兼畜人，小国不过欲入事人。

夫两者各得其所欲，大者宜为下。

Chapter 61. Win-Win Diplomacy

A big State should flow down (humbly) like a stream. It should be humble under Heaven, like females.

The females eternally vanquish the males through Stillness.
Therefore, if a big State deprecates itself before a small State, then it could win (loyalty) from the small State.
If a small State deprecates itself before a big State, then it could win (concession) from the big State.
Therefore, either self-deprecation is intended to win over others; or, self-deprecation has the bonus side effect of winning over others.
A big State succeeds by uniting and nurturing people. A small State succeeds by serving others.
In order for both to win-win, the big State might better self-deprecate.

Notes:

The author continued to address a ruler of a big state in ancient China. He compared the big state to a female which makes reader suspect either the ruler of the big state was a dowager queen or the particular ruler was strongly influenced by a female member of family.

Either way, Dao De Jing throughout mentioned Mothers and women with respect, spoke highly of their resilience, persistence and nurturing nature.

The author suggested diplomatic policies that take into both sides' interest and win-win thinking. The best diplomacy policy is to self-deprecate. No arrogance, no bragging, no threats, no intrigues, no deception.

第六十二章 道为天下贵

道者万物之奥，善人之宝，

不善人之所保。

美言可以市尊，美行可以加

人。

人之不善，何弃之有？

故立天子，置三公，虽有拱

璧以先驷马，不如坐进此

道。

古之所以贵此道者何？

不曰求以得？

有罪以免邪！

故为天下贵。

Chapter 62. Guardian and Redemption

The Dao is the Mystery of ten thousand things. It is treasured by the masters, yet it is also guardian of the noobs.

Pretty words could trade-in for honors, Good deeds could bring admirers.

Some people are incapable of such, (that's normal), so why abandon them?
Therefore, when the Son of Heaven (the Emperor) assumes his position, he appoints his standard three Dukes, even if he procures his official jade emblem and his four horse-carriage team, he should instead sit back, and pay homage to this Dao.
Why did the ancients prize this Dao so much?

Is it not because, he who seeks it will achieve (Enlightenment)?
Even, he who is guilty could still be redeemed through Dao!
Therefore, (Dao) becomes the most prized under Heaven.

Notes:

Laozi offered more suggestions to the big state's leader. Dao means to protect, to enlighten and to redeem. Dao forms a basis for legislation and constitution.

His argument goes as follows:
1) Pretty words and good deeds are all tradable assets and represent artifice. (These are Ritualist virtues).
2) All people were once noobs, before they turn into masters of pretty words and good deeds. Some people may never be capable of pretty words and good deeds. More importantly, pretty words and good deeds often are misleading (Chapter 81), while truth often come out of the mouth of babes.
3) Hence all people, even in their natural unschooled uncouth stage, have inherent dignity and access to truth.
4) Therefore, even noobs or guilty people are worthy of protection, enlightenment and redemption.

Laozi warned against thought-policing, morality-policing and spoke against such overreach. Subsequently, in history, Confucian dynasties would often penalize free speech and nonconformists, even using capital punishment.

第六十三章 轻诺必寡信

dì liù shí sān zhāng qīng nuò bì guǎ xìn

wéi wú wéi， shì wú shì， wèi wú wèi。
为无为，事无事，味无味。

dà xiǎo duō shǎo （bào yuàn yǐ dé*）：
大小多少（报怨以德*）：

tú nán yú qí yì， wéi dà yú qí xì。
图难于其易，为大于其细。

tiān xià nán shì， bì zuò yú yì； tiān xià
天下难事，必作于易；天下

dà shì， bì zuò yú xì。
大事，必作于细。

shì yǐ shèng rén zhōng bù wéi dà， gù néng chéng
是以圣人终不为大，故能成

qí dà。
其大。

fū qīng nuò bì guǎ xìn， duō yì bì duō
夫轻诺必寡信，多易必多

nàn。
难。

shì yǐ shèng rén yóu nán zhī， gù zhōng wú nán
是以圣人犹难之，故终无难

yǐ。
矣。

Chapter 63. Over-Promise Under-Deliver

Act without (appearing to) act, serve without (appearing to) serve, savor without (preferring a particular) flavor.

Big and small, many and few (*):
in planning, difficulties must be anticipated even while the project appears easy; in action, the big projects depend on small details.

All difficult projects under Heaven, must be accomplished through easy steps; all big projects, must be accomplished through attention to detail.

Therefore, the Sage usually avoid tackling big projects in big chunks, therefore he could accomplish the big (projects).

Because over-promise necessitates under-delivery, (reckless) assumption of ease necessitates surprise difficulties.

Therefore, the Sage treads cautiously, anticipates difficulty, hence, (he) completes (projects) without difficulty.

Notes:
This chapter talks about project management, to be continued in the next chapter. How to estimate the difficulty of a project? How to estimate the impact and scale of a project? There are two options:
1) Over promise, under deliver
2) Under promise, over deliver (Laozi's suggestion)

Some people claim that Laozi tailored his advices for a small city state's ruler. However, I do not think evidence points to this conclusion. Quite the opposite:
1) Laozi repeatedly spoke of scaling problems, only a big organization and big state would have to face problems with scale. Simplicity in laws, neutral administration, complex projects are relevant to big state, but not necessary for a tiny city state where everyone knows everyone else.
2) Laozi repeatedly gave advice for big states and kings and emperor explicitly. Being unusually reticent and circumspect, Laozi was unlikely to give unsolicited advice to royalty whom he did not know personally.
3) Within 100 years, Laozi's philosophy was widely practiced in many of the biggest and most successful states in ancient China during the Warring States period.
4) Within 1000 years, Laozi's philosophy played a central role, in building the most powerful, most effective, most liberal dynasties in Chinese History (early Han, Tang, Eastern Jin Dynasty). This was very good record for any organizational scaling principle.

(抱怨以德) *: does not fit in the context. Many suspects it fits better in Chapter 79. So, I move it there.

dì liù shí sì zhāng　shèn zhōng rú shǐ
第六十四章　慎终如始

qí ān yì chí　　qí wèi zhào yì móu
其安易持；其未兆易谋。

qí cuì yì pàn　　qí wēi yì sàn
其脆易泮；其微易散。

wéi zhī yú wèi yǒu
为之于未有，

zhì zhī yú wèi luàn
治之于未乱。

hé bào zhī mù　　shēng yú háo mò
合抱之木，生于毫末；

jiǔ céng zhī tái　　qǐ yú lěi tǔ
九层之台，起于垒土；

qiān lǐ zhī xíng　　shǐ yú zú xià
千里之行，始于足下。

wéi zhě bài zhī　　zhí zhě shī zhī
为者败之，执者失之。

shì yǐ　shèng rén wú wéi　gù wú bài
是以，圣人无为，故无败；

wú zhí　　gù wú shī
无执，故无失。

mín zhī cóng shì　　cháng yú jǐ chéng ér bài
民之从事，常于几成而败

zhī
之。

shèn zhōng rú shǐ　　zé wú bài shì
慎终如始，则无败事。

shì yǐ　shèng rén yù bù yù　　bù guì nán
是以，圣人欲不欲，不贵难

dé zhī huò　　xué bù xué　　fù zhòng rén zhī
得之货，学不学，复众人之

suǒ guò
所过。

yǐ fǔ wàn wù zì rán ér bù gǎn wéi
以辅万物自然而不敢为。

Chapter 64. Foresight and Persistence

A stable system is sensitive to maneuvering; if disasters are caught before manifestations, they are easy to avert.
While still fragile, (threats) are easily broken up; while still microscopic, (chaos) is easily dispersed.
Act before full blown manifestations, bring order before full blown chaos.

A stout tree trunk, began in a tiny seed.

Nine story high platform, was originally a small pile of dirt.
Journey of a thousand Li (*Chinese miles*), began in stepping out one foot.
People who act with fanfare, will be thwarted (before reaching critical mass). People who hold onto control, will be deprived (because seeds of resistance will grow through the cracks).
Therefore, the Sage does not act with fanfare, so he is not thwarted. He does not hold on to control, so he is not deprived.
Ordinary people, starting a job, often give up midway.

If they are cautious all the way to completion, like how they first started up, then they could have avoided these half-baked failures.
Therefore, the Sage prefers no preference, devalues the valuable goods, mimics no mimic, carefully goes over the mistakes by everybody.

Thus, he helps all things to follow their own nature, and dares not Interfere.

Notes:

Once again, Laozi put on his historian's hat. "prefers no preference, devalue the valuable, mimic no mimic, carefully go over the mistakes by everybody". This chapter continues Chapter 59, in explaining typical systems based on feed-forward loops. These systems either grow or shrink, their changes may not be visible yet rapid, they are difficult to control and hold steady.

This chapter moved through several related lessons:

1. Foresight of the bad omens, when changes are underway. （其安易持。。。）
2. Seed of hope that starts a worthy venture. On the flip side, seed of threats also may grow. (合抱之木，九层之台，千里之行)
3. Avoid fanfare that alerts opponents of your projects before you reach critical mass; （无为故无败）
4. Also avoid instinct to micromanage and over-control. Because no matter how hard you try, some threats will grow through the cracks. The more controlling you are, the worse their resistance. (无执故无失)
5. How to persist to completion (民之从事，常于几成而败之)
6. Develop individual value system (欲无欲，不贵难得之货)
7. Develop individual style with critical thinking and learning from mistakes (学无学，复众人之所过)
8. Ultimately the goal is to help everything follow their nature, instead of fulfilling someone's own vanity and wish to control （以辅万物自然）

合抱之木：a tree trunk that requires multiple persons link arms to embrace
里：measure of transportation distance, probably equals a little less than ½ kilometer.
几成：一成 means 10%；10%-90%,

第六十五章 善为道者

古之善为道者，非以明民，将以愚之。

民之难治，以其智多。

故以智治国，国之贼；

不以智治国，国之福。

知此两者亦稽式。

常知稽式，是谓玄德。

玄德深矣，远矣，与物反矣，然后乃至大顺。

Chapter 65. Decision Science

Rulers in the ancient times followed the Dao, not by "educating" their people, but by making their people "foolish".

People are unruly, because they are too clever.

Hence, if a State promote "cleverness", this State is soon stolen.
If a State reject "cleverness", this State is blessed.

He who knows these two (choices), understand the art of decision making.
He who understand the art of sustainable decision making, has the Profound Virtue (De).
Profound Virtue is profound, is far reaching, but is contrary to simple intuition, therefore (intuition and counter-intuition) will unite to usher in the big Order.

Notes:

This chapter has a Legalist overtone. It also does not fit well in the context. Some suspect that Legalist scholars added it. However, it's also possible later Legalists took this chapter and carried it to extremes of "愚民" (fooling the people, depriving people of education and freedom of speech), thus, violating the intent of the original author Laozi.

Laozi's "fooling the people" should be instead be interpreted as the following:
Laozi consistently disclaimed the idea of cleverness/ trickery / artifice "智", especially standards proclaiming such artificial, unnecessary and complex virtues. Ultimately, this supposed virtue (cleverness / trickery / artifice) promote complexity and fragility in a complex societal system, also they make the complex system difficult to scale in size, to handle massive projects routinely; those people who advocate these standards, will soon cause extreme swings and collapse.
Humans constitute societies to ward off threats and chaos. Society rules should be simple and true. But instead, virtues (like intelligence and beauty) routinely game the system. Instead of straight talk, "clever" people lie and cover up their lies through extra layers of complexity. The more people are rewarded for such virtues, the more systems will break.

Instead, the author in Chapter 20, self-deprecated as ("愚") foolish and dull, therefore an example of true "education" and true "enlightenment" that allowed people to follow their own nature and speak true. Laozi in this chapter advocated the same for all people, thus, Daoism is the opposite of Legalism's extreme misinterpretation. Choices of standardization and conformity could make or break an organization.

Later part of this chapter spoke of 稽式, *Dao De Jing* was a toolbox for science, leadership and decision making, intuitive and counter-intuitive decision making.
稽式: Choices, decisions, rules

dì liù shí liù zhāng   mò néng yǔ zhēng
第六十六章 莫能与争

jiāng hǎi zhī suǒ yǐ néng wéi bǎi gǔ wáng zhě
江海之所以能为百谷王者，
yǐ qí shàn xià zhī   gù néng wéi bǎi gǔ
以其善下之，故能为百谷
wáng
王。

shì yǐ shèng rén yù shàng mín   bì yǐ yán xià
是以圣人欲上民，必以言下
zhī   yù xiān mín   bì yǐ shēn hòu zhī
之；欲先民，必以身后之。

shì yǐ shèng rén chù shàng ér mín bù zhòng   chù
是以圣人处上而民不重，处
qián ér mín bù hài
前而民不害。

shì yǐ tiān xià lè tuī ér bù yàn
是以天下乐推而不厌。
yǐ qí bù zhēng   gù tiān xià mò néng yǔ zhī
以其不争，故天下莫能与之
zhēng
争。

Chapter 66. No-Rivalry and No Rivals

Why are rivers and oceans called kings of all valleys?

Because they lie low, therefore, they are kings of all valleys.

Similarly, if the Sage want to lead from top, he must speak from the bottom; if he wants to be the first, he must follow.

Thus, when eventually the Sage end up on top, people will not be oppressed; when the Sage end up in front, then people will not be injured.

Therefore, all people under Heaven are willing to help him, not grow tired of him.
Because he offers No-Rivalry, therefore no one under Heaven could rival him.

Notes:

When an organization is built on No-Rivalry, internal frictions and seeds of distrust do not grow and escalate. Thus, the organization is set on a path of sustainable success.

Because Laozi's audience seemed to be leaders and rulers, his words (不争) took on a particular meaning, No-Rivalry means "no monopolies". In ancient China, governments meddled into marketplace to gain mainly through monopolies, police power, taxes and tariffs. Laozi would speak out against all these interferences.

The basis of No-Rivalry, is actually the radically simplified value system outlined throughout *Dao De Jing*. They are all connected:
1. Individual value system (欲无欲，不贵难得之货)
2. Mimic no mimic. (学无学，not copying others success)
3. Simplicity and honesty (朴,素)
4. Foolishness (愚)
5. Beneficial like life-saving Water (上善若水，常善救人,慈)
6. Neutrality and conflict resolution (无常心，挫其锐，解其纷)
7. No-interference, no showoffs, no control freaks （无为，无见，无执）
8. Avoid militarism and escalation (兵者不祥之器，勇于不敢)
9. Self knowledge, self-love, self-sufficiency, self-governance (自知，自爱，自足，自立，自化)
10. Separation of powers (不敢代大匠斲)

第六十七章 我有三宝

天下皆谓我道大，似不肖。

夫唯大，故似不肖。

若肖，久矣其细也夫。

我有三宝，持而保之：

一曰慈，二曰俭，三曰不敢为天下先。

慈故能勇，俭故能广，不敢为天下先，故能成器长。

今舍慈且勇，舍俭且广，舍后且先；死矣。

夫慈以战则胜；以守则固。

天将救之，以慈卫之。

Chapter 67. Three Treasures of Dao

Everyone under Heaven tells me that Dao is too big, it is like nothing else (hence, not intuitive). Exactly that it is too big, therefore it's like nothing else.

If it is like other things, then it would have long since worn out.

I have three treasures, that I cherish always:

The first is Love. The second is Simplicity. The third is not daring being the First under Heaven.

Love leads to Courage. Simplicity leads to (massive) Scale. Not daring claims of being the First under Heaven, leads to Resilience.

Today, (people) give up love to (maintain) Courage, give up Simplicity to scale massively, give up following others to lead; such mistakes are deadly.

Love, in battle, will triumph; in defense, (Love) will endure.

When Heaven will save us, it first protects us through Love.

Notes:

This key chapter brings multiple chapters together. At first Laozi seemed to be responding to audience's concern: "Dao is so vague and incomprehensible, too big". He answered that Dao is big, and it is also sustainable, scalable and resilient.

Then he offered three treasures that will helps sustainable, scalable and resilient practice of Dao. These treasures were explained elsewhere, but in this chapter, he emphasized the parental (especially maternal) Love (慈), and explained why this mundane virtue of ordinary humans, could guide them to Heroic Courage and Divine Blessings.

The 2nd treasure: Simplicity was explained in context
The 3rd treasure: No-Rivalry was explained in context, especially the next chapter

dì liù shí bā zhāng bù zhēng zhī dé
第六十八章 不争之德

shàn wéi shì zhě   bù wǔ
善为士者，不武。

shàn zhàn zhě   bù nù
善战者，不怒。

shàn shèng dí zhě   bù yǔ
善胜敌者，不与。

shàn yòng rén zhě   wéi zhī xià
善用人者，为之下。

shì wèi bù zhēng zhī dé   shì wèi yòng rén zhī
是谓不争之德，是谓用人之

lì   shì wèi pèi tiān   gǔ zhī jí
力，是谓配天，古之极。

Chapter 68. No-Rivalry Complementing Heaven

Masterful gentlemen are not brutal.

Masterful warriors are not enraged.

Masterful generals, do not give away advantage.
Masterful leaders, self-deprecate.

This is called the Virtue (De) of No-Rivalry. This is called the (efficient) application of human resource. This is called complementing Heaven, the ultimate ancient (wisdom).

Notes:

Continued expansion of the 3rd treasure. No-Rivalry is important to reduce friction and wearing, within an institution. It is also important to reduce external frictions.

The audience were composed of both civilian and war leaders.

用人：human resource, leadership

第六十九章 哀者胜矣

用兵有言："吾不敢为主而为客，不敢进寸而退尺。"

是谓行无行，攘无臂，扔无敌，执无兵。

祸莫大于轻敌，轻敌几丧吾宝。

故抗兵相若，哀者胜矣。

Chapter 69. Triumph of the Underdog

(I) quote from a military leader: "I dare not to be the host but consider myself a guest, I dare not to advance an inch but withdraw a foot."

Such is advancing no advances, grabbing without arms, hitting without enemy forces, controlling without soldiers.

The worst disasters come from underestimating enemy threats, by underestimating threats I almost lost my three treasures.
Therefore, when two opposing armies are evenly matched, the desperate side, will triumph.

Notes:

This chapter is personal chapter. Especially when the author spoke of "by underestimating threats I almost lost my three treasures".

Laozi might have worked as a war historian and even might have eye-witnessed some battles. We know nothing of his younger days, when he could have been a soldier, a military leader or a war reporter, similar to Socrates. He probably underestimated a weaker but more desperate opponent, or at least witnessed some such defeats.

This chapter was addressed to war leaders and might have inspired other war classics such as Sun-zi.

哀者: the wronged party, the aggrieved party, the chronic underdogs, the desperate

第七十章 言有宗

dì qī shí zhāng yán yǒu zōng

吾言甚易知，甚易行。
wú yán shèn yì zhī shèn yì xíng

天下莫能知，莫能行。
tiān xià mò néng zhī mò néng xíng

言有宗，事有君。
yán yǒu zōng shì yǒu jūn

夫唯无知，是以不我知。
fū wéi wú zhī shì yǐ bù wǒ zhī

知我者希，则我者贵。
zhī wǒ zhě xī zé wǒ zhě guì

是以圣人被褐而怀玉。
shì yǐ shèng rén bèi hè ér huái yù

Chapter 70. Backed by Evidence

My words are easy to know, and easy to practice.
Yet few under Heaven could know, and few could practice.
My words are backed by evidence, they serve practical purpose.
Only because people lack in knowledge, they do not understand me.
People who know me are rare, who follow my teachings will be exalted.
Similarly, the Sage wears coarse fabric, yet hold (precious) jade to their bosoms.

Notes:

The key to this chapter and the next three chapters, is knowledge "知" and practice "行" "事" "则".

Laozi was winding down from this point. He rarely uses big words, but instead kept his language simple. He wanted his message simple, honest, helpful and accessible. From a long life, he also realized that the actual world (even in his age) appear to prefer the opposites: the complex, the beautiful, the vain, the deceptive, the deadly. This phenomenon is now called "bad money drives out good"- Gresham's Law.

Throughout the book, the author seemed to be talking to someone, as now:
  Q: are these words or knowledge coming from somewhere?
  A: they came from many sources, they are backed by evidence. 言有宗.
  Q: do these words serve any practical purpose?
  A: they serve practical purposes. 事有君. Laozi is very practical minded.
  Q: Is knowledge easier or practice easier?
  A: What I say is easy to understand and easy to practice. However, few people understand or practice.
  Q: Why is this?
  A: Truth does not compete with cosmetics.

Then the author continued to defend his thesis based on his copious historic evidence.
Unfortunately, Laozi's source evidence, up to 1000year worth of Chinese written histories (from Shang Dynasty and Zhou Dynasty), did not survive long. About 300 years later after Laozi's book, during Qin Dynasty legalist regime and subsequent civil war, almost all pre-Qin and Qin Dynasty records were destroyed. Subsequently, during early Han emperors' Daoist reign, previous records were partially collected and restored. Daoist scholar Sima Tan and his son, Sima Qian(司马迁), gained access to these partial records through their court historian position, thus *The Histories* 《史记》 was born.

Dao De Jing, the book, was widely copied during its first 300 years in publication. But it also met the same fate as its "sources", was banned and almost lost during the Qin Dynasty. Thankfully the Qin Dynasty was short-lived (20 years or so). Early Han Emperors actively sought out surviving Daoist scholars to bring *Dao De Jing* back into publication. Laozi's principles guided Han Dynasty Administration in China's recovery from ravages of tyranny and civil wars.

第七十一章 以其病病

知不知，上；不知知，病。

夫唯病病，是以不病。

圣人不病，以其病病。

Chapter 71. Knowledge of the Unknown

Knowing what (you) do not know, this is the highest (virtue); Not knowing (the limit to) what (you) know, this is problematic.

Only if (you) know the problem as problematic, therefore (you) could avoid the problem.

The Sage avoids the problem, by identifying it.

Notes:

Chapters 70,71,72,73 all deals with knowledge in different aspects. This chapter refers to problem diagnostics type knowledge as medical diagnosis.

Limits to knowledge, needs to be honestly acknowledged. People do not know what they do not know. Most people do not identify a problem as a problem. Key steps are to know:

1) Limit to knowledge
2) How to identify problems
3) How to avert complications and prevent problems

Dao De Jing was published, was widely copied and inspired a long line of Chinese medical doctors and scientists in scientific pursuits.

Many of Dao De Jing's passages, appears scattered and diluted in Confucian Canons (which was collected and published much later). Perhaps this was a case of intellectual knock-off, perhaps all were innocent as wisdom from a common source. Coincidences are worth paying attention to.

病： disease, problems

第七十二章 无狎其所居

民不畏威，则大威至。

无狎其所居，无厌其所生。

夫唯不厌，是以不厌。

是以圣人自知不自见，自爱不自贵。

故去彼取此。

Chapter 72. Do Not Pry

When people are not awed by authorities, then the big authority is in place.
Do not pry into their private lives, do not deprive them of livelihoods.
Only when (authorities) do not harass its people, then the people will not tire of (authorities).
Therefore, the Sage knows himself without showing off, loves himself without self-glorification.
So, (he) avoids that (showing off and self-glorification) and follows this (self-knowledge and self-love).

Notes:

This chapter continues "知" knowledge discussion, but seems to restrain eager leaders from prying.

The first sentence has a reasonable alternative translation, particularly combined with Chapter 74:
When people are not afraid of threats (威), then great peril will come (after the ruler).

This chapter advised the authorities to take a laissez-faire approach, respecting privacy and free market approach in economics. This advice is far different from Legalistic approach, or the Confucian approach.

Do not pry into their private lives, do not deprive of their livelihoods. Live and let live. Authorities must exercise restraint.

These were ancient legislative principles prevalent in Chinese Daoist dynasties. They were comparable to the US Constitution.

第七十三章 天网恢恢

勇于敢则杀，勇于不敢则活。

此两者，或利或害。

天之所恶，孰知其故？

是以圣人犹难之。

天之道，不争而善胜，不言而善应，不召而自来，繟然而善谋。

天网恢恢，疏而不漏。

Chapter 73. Heaven's Net Justice

Courage that is based on daring will end in Death, Courage that is based on restraint will end in Life.

These two strategies, (daring and restraint), will either benefit or injure.
Heaven seems to punish certain strategies, who knows why?
Therefore, the Sage knows the difficulty in this strategy choice.
(The Sage with) Heaven's Dao, avoids rivalry yet reaches victory, avoids big talk yet reaches consensus, (his help is) uncalled for, yet (he) comes to help by his own volition, (he is) laid back yet he plans ahead.

The Heaven's Justice is like a vast net, it is sparse but inescapable.

Notes:

This chapter continues "知" knowledge discussion and echoes Chapter 50's strategy choices, especially about tough choices between daring and restraint.

天之所恶. 孰知其故：This sentence is continuation of Chapter 71 (知不知). Difficult strategy choices also involve another important question in history: cause-and-effect. What caused what? Why some strategies prosper? Why other strategies lead to disasters? Cause-and-effect were the most difficult questions in history. Almost all people, even learned historians got them wrong. Unrelated coincidences were mistaken for causes; correlation were mistaken for causes; effects were mistaken for causes; falsified events were mistaken for causes. Laozi quite plainly pointed out: the true causes are often unknown, may be unknowable. But knowing the unknown （知不知）, is a step in the right direction.

Eventually, the last sentences echoes Ancients call of Heaven's Justice, symbolized by a fishing net.

	Positioned to Live(生地)	Positioned to Die(死地)
Live(生)	3/10 the Lucky Lottery Winners （生之徒，勇于不敢）	1/10 the Survivors of Anything （善摄生者，其无死地，勇于不敢）
Die(死)	3/10 the Profligate Losers （以其生生之厚，勇于敢） **Chapter 53**	3/10 the Unlucky Losers （死之徒，勇于敢）

Again, these were ancient criminal justice principles prevalent in Chinese Daoist dynasties. Comparable to the US Constitution.

第七十四章 代大匠斲

民不畏死，奈何以死惧之？

若使民常畏死，

而为奇者，

吾得执而杀之，孰敢？

常有司杀者杀，夫代司杀者

杀，是谓代大匠斲。

夫代大匠斲者，希有不伤其

手矣。

Chapter 74. Separation of Power

When (criminal) people are no longer afraid of Death, why threaten them with Death?

If (criminal) people are afraid of Death, as Death is rare and unnatural, then I, (the police authorities), only go after the exceptionally dangerous criminals and execute them, then who will risk challenging (the police)? Ultimately the judicial authorities are responsible of criminal execution. If other branches try to execute (criminals) instead, this is (extra-judicial over-reach) like replacing a master craftsman in his dangerous trade. When someone decide to replace a master craftsman in his dangerous trade, he almost always (*double negative*) hurt his own hand.

Notes:

This chapter is continuation of Chapter 73. Laozi turned clearly to address police and judicial power, maybe police and judicial officers were present in the audience.

First, he outlined the problems of overzealous officials and over-harsh legal codes.
Then, he suggested that judicial powers to devote more resources to the exceptionally dangerous, instead of the minor offenders.
Finally, he advocated a clean separation of powers: judicial and non-judicial. As earlier, he advocated the separation of military and civilian in Chapter 31.

Again, *Dao De Jing*, embodies governance principles prevalent in Chinese Daoist dynasties, is comparable to the US Constitution. Laozi from his study of history, arrived at the same conclusions as the American Founding Fathers: separation of powers is essential to sustainable government.

第七十五章 贵生
dì qī shí wǔ zhāng guì shēng

民之饥，以其上食税之多，
mín zhī jī, yǐ qí shàng shí shuì zhī duō,

是以饥。
shì yǐ jī.

民之难治，以其上之有为，
mín zhī nán zhì, yǐ qí shàng zhī yǒuwéi,

是以难治。
shì yǐ nán zhì.

民之轻死，以其上求生之
mín zhī qīng sǐ, yǐ qí shàng qiúshēng zhī

厚，是以轻死。
hòu, shì yǐ qīng sǐ.

夫唯无以生为者，是贤于贵
fū wéi wú yǐ shēng wéi zhě, shì xián yú guì

生。
shēng.

Chapter 75. Value of Life

People become hungry, when their rulers tax too much, hence the hunger.

People become unruly, when their rulers Interfere too much, hence the unruliness.

People become reckless of Death, when their rulers value their own lives and control too much (at their expense), hence the recklessness.

Only when the rulers stop valuing their own lives and their control (ahead of their people's livelihood), then (their strategy) is more sustainable than valuing their own lives directly.

Notes:

This chapter turns to the taxation, police power, mutual trust between the governed and government.

This chapter echoes Chapter 50's game theory, especially expounding on the square where people or organizations that should have lived, actually entered into a death spiral. Why? they tax, they police, they go to extremes, they push their people into uncertainty and desperation.

Again, Laozi from his study of history, arrived at the same conclusions as the American Founding Fathers: individual rights must be protected and government powers must be restrained.

	Positioned to Live(生地)	Positioned to Die(死地)
Live(生)	3/10 the Lucky Lottery Winners （生之徒）	1/10 the Survivors of Anything （善摄生者，其无死地）Chapter 50,55
Die(死)	**3/10 the Profligate Losers** （以其生生之厚）**Chapter 53**	3/10 the Unlucky Losers （死之徒）

第七十六章 柔弱处上

人之生也柔弱，其死也坚强。

万物草木之生也柔脆，其死也枯槁。

故坚强者死之徒，柔弱者生之徒。

是以兵强则不胜，木强则折。

强大处下，柔弱处上。

Chapter 76. Weak and Flexible Will Triumph

People are born soft and flexible, yet they die stiffened and strong.

All things like grass and woods are born soft and flexible, they die dry and withered.

Therefore, the stiffened and strong belong to Death, while the soft and flexible belong to Life.

Therefore, strong armies will not conquer, the strong lumber will fracture.

The powerful goes down, the soft and flexible goes on top.

Notes:

This chapter expands Chapter 50's game theory on the hidden counterintuitive rules behind Life and Death squares.

This chapter also continued Chapter 75, to advocate the restraint in government powers, especially use of violence. As consequence of power abuse, Laozi predicted disastrous collapse (木强则折). In the 2500-year history since *Dao De Jing* was written, examples abound.

Instead, resilience and sustainability are the keys to survival and triumph.

	Positioned to Live(生地)	Positioned to Die(死地)
Live(生)	3/10 the Lucky Lottery Winners （生之徒）	**1/10 the Survivors of Anything （善摄生者，其无死地）Chapter 50,55**
Die(死)	**3/10 the Profligate Losers （以其生生之厚） Chapter 53**	3/10 the Unlucky Losers （死之徒）

第七十七章 天人之道

天之道，其犹张弓欤？

高者抑之，下者举之；

有余者损之，

不足者补之。

天之道，损有余而补不足。

人之道，则不然；损不足以

奉有余。

孰能有余以奉天下？ 唯有道

者。

是以圣人为而不恃，功成而

不处，其不欲见贤。

Chapter 77. Different Dao

The Dao of Heaven, is it not like aiming a drawn bow?
From the high point, the arrow-man aims low, from the low point, the arrow-man aims high;
at extra (close) range, the arrow-man reduces (the bow's power).
At insufficient (farther) range, the arrow-man supplements the bow's power.
Thus, the Dao of Heaven, reduces the extra, supplements the insufficient.
The Dao of humans, is the opposite; it reduces the insufficient to supplement those who already enjoys extra.

Who could use the extra to supplement all under Heaven? Only the people with Dao.

Therefore, the Sage serves without possessiveness, completes his mission without dwelling on his accomplishments. He does not wish to show off his (excess) virtues.

Notes:

This chapter is about the difference between Heaven's Dao vs Human Dao.
Heaven's Dao is better at redistribution. It runs like entropy and naturally trends to equilibrium. (Thermodynamics). It also practices "return to the Norm". See Chapter 32.
In human affairs, by contrast, wealth and even virtues often become over-concentrated in a few. The tug and pull of both Dao, if unchecked, often end violently; when Heaven's Dao show its invisible hands, through upheavals and revolutions, people are caught by surprise.

So, the leaders should be aware of both Dao algorithms, the human algorithm and especially the hidden counter-intuitive Heaven's Dao.

第七十八章 正言若反

天下莫柔弱于水，而攻坚强者莫之能胜，以其无以易之。

弱之胜强，柔之胜刚，天下莫不知，莫能行。

是以圣人云：受国之垢，是谓社稷主。

受国之不祥，是为天下王。

正言若反。

Chapter 78. Truth seems Contrary

Nothing under Heaven is softer and more flexible than Water, yet the strongest things fail to prevail over Water, because Water is so irreplaceable.

The soft prevails over the strong, the flexible prevails over the hardened. Everyone under Heaven know this Truth (*double negative*), but few will follow it to action.

Therefore, the Sage said: (he who) receives the nation's dirt, becomes the King of the nation.

(He who) receives inauspicious omens under Heaven, he becomes the King under Heaven. Truth seems contrary (to intuition).

Notes:

A key insight from Laozi: feedback loops modulate/moderate the behavior of a complex system.

The humbly benign, will eventually triumph over their more violently destructive counterparts.

Ancient rulers in China (before Laozi's time) were often themselves Cassandras, versed in oracles. The historic records they left behind formed bases for Laozi's insights.

Foresight, insights, common sense, critical thinking, contrarian, following them to action, these traits are uncommon gifts even today.

第七十九章 常与善人
dì qī shí jiǔ zhāng cháng yǔ shàn rén

和大怨，必有余怨，
hé dà yuàn，bì yǒu yú yuàn

报怨以德*，
bào yuàn yǐ dé

安可以为善？
ān kěyǐ wéi shàn

是以圣人执左契，
shì yǐ shèng rén zhí zuǒ qì

而不责于人。
ér bù zé yú rén

有德司契，
yǒu dé sī qì

无德司彻。
wú dé sī chè

天道无亲，
tiān dào wú qīn

常与善人。
cháng yǔ shàn rén

Chapter 79. Contracts and Neutral Arbiter

(Even if people) make peace after holding great grudge, there will surely be more resentments.
(Some suggest that we should) pay back grudges with kindness*; but how then could (we) proceed to make sustainable peace?

Therefore, the Sage hold on to left half of contract, (as the owner of debt),
but he does not force people to honor the contract (to extremes).
People with Virtue (*De*) governs by contracts (evidence of contracts), people without Virtue (*De*) governs by extreme force.
The Dao of Heaven has no (familial or tribal) preference,
but often yield to people that could sustainably follow Dao.

Notes:

This chapter covers the topics of forgiveness vs vengeance, peace vs violence:

1) Making peace after internal strife, would-be peacemakers need to be aware that wounds are raw, and that resentments are wide spread.
2) Chapter 63 has a sentence that might fit better here. "抱怨以德".
   In other words, there are many types of grudges and resentments, they require fine-tuned response, how could a single response "抱怨以德" suffice to fit all of them? Suffering like a saint silently is not exactly recommended here.
3) To answer the above questions, Laozi suggested a contractual system where the leader acts as a contract recorder, a mediator or an arbitrator.
4) While authorities should be neutral to tribes or family clans, cumulatively on average, Heaven's Dao, tend to favor people who sustainably practice Dao.

Some scholars think that the left side of the contract means the liable side. In context, I feel the debt holder side is closer to original meaning.

This chapter formed the legal and religious principles underlying compromises and peace-making in Daoism. The Chinese Daoist dynasties (early Han, Easter Jin, Tang) used these principles to reach post-civil-war compromises.

dì bā shí zhāng xiǎo guó guǎ mín
第八十章 小国寡民

xiǎo guó guǎ mín
小国寡民。

shǐ yǒu shén bó zhī qì
使有什伯之器

ér bú yòng
而不用。

shǐ mín zhòng sǐ ér bù yuǎn xǐ
使民重死而不远徙。

suī yǒu zhōu yú   wú suǒ chéng zhī
虽有舟舆，无所乘之。

suī yǒu jiǎ bīng   wú suǒ chén zhī
虽有甲兵，无所陈之。

shǐ mín fù jié shéng ér yòng zhī
使民复结绳而用之。

gān qí shí   měi qí fú
甘其食，美其服，

ān qí jū   lè qí sú
安其居，乐其俗。

lín guó xiāng wàng   jī quǎn zhī shēng xiāng wén
邻国相望，鸡犬之声相闻，

mín zhì lǎo sǐ   bù xiāng wǎng lái
民至老死，不相往来。

Chapter 80. Independence and Self-Sufficiency

Small nations with few people (are ideal).

Even though they own tools ten or hundred times as powerful, they do not use the tools.

Their people find Death heavy and they are not driven out to far-away ventures (by poor governance).
Thus, even though the people have access to boats and carriages, they do not jump aboard.
Even though the people own weapons and soldiers, they need not line out in battle.
Eventually their people return to Simplicity, using rope knots to record their history.
They enjoy their food, tidy up their apparel, keep safe their homes, treasure their traditions.

Neighboring States could sight each other, hear each other's chicken and dogs; yet their people would turn grey and die, with self-sufficiency, never bother to visit back and forth.

Notes:

The author increasingly sounded like a cranky old neighbor. Laozi was probably born when China still had many tiny municipalities and enjoyed some pastoral peace in his youth. He lived a long life to witness these municipalities fall apart. Yet his dream of a world full of self-sufficient and independent utopias rung true to his time, and still ring true today. Think Switzerland and Sweden, think New Zealand, even think of some of the original thirteen American colonies.

Simplicity, honesty, self-sufficiency, tradition, security, environmental sustainability, these were simple values. Yet they are often abandoned in quest of the complex, deception, big, modernity, globalization, profits and power grab.

Refer to the US Constitution for many similarities.

第八十一章 信言不美
dì bā shí yī zhāng xìn yán bù měi

信言不美，美言不信。
xìn yán bù měi   měi yán bù xìn

善者不辩，辩者不善。
shàn zhě bù biàn   biàn zhě bú shàn

知者不博，博者不知。
zhī zhě bù bó   bó zhě bù zhī

圣人不积，既以为人己愈
shèng rén bù jī   jì yǐ wéi rén jǐ yù

有；既以与人己愈多。
yǒu   jì yǐ yǔ rén jǐ yù duō

天之道，利而不害；
tiān zhī dào   lì ér bù hài

圣人之道，为而不争。
shèng rén zhī dào   wéi ér bù zhēng

Chapter 81. Paradoxes of Honesty

Honest words lack beauty. Beautiful words lack Honesty.
Good people do not debate. Debaters are not that good.
Wise people are not all-knowing. All-knowing people are not wise.
A Sage does not accumulate, because the more he serves others, the more he owns; the more he gives to others, the more he gets.

Heaven's Dao, does benefit and does not injure.

The Sage practices Dao, by serving without Rivalry.

Notes:

Dao De Jing opened with paradoxes, and it closed with paradoxes.
1) "信言不美，美言不信" connects to Chapter 1 "道可道非常道" and Chapter 2. "天下皆知美之为美者". A paradox of standardization/conformity and economics. In economics, Gresham's law is a monetary principle stating that "bad money drives out good". The same phenomenon happens in marketplace for people and for thoughts. Laozi seemed to have noticed and predicted that this paradox would influence the history. And it did, many times.
2) 信言不美，美言不信. Also, this is a logical paradox. Beauty (on the surface) and Honesty (to the core) may be fundamentally contradictory.
3) 信言不美，美言不信. Laozi tended to be very pragmatic. "Beauty" seemed to imply complexity or beautifully worded communication. This sentence may also be admonition against 1) when people use complexity to gain advantage and game systems; 2) when people expect to hear the good news couched in flowery language only and even shoot the messenger of bad news but true information. Both behaviors, would go on to influence history and cause many disasters.
4) "圣人不积" connects to Chapter 77. the Leader must be neutral, thus minimize conflict of interest. Hence he must not accumulate the commonly accepted currency (money, power, fame, etc), but instead accumulate understanding and practice of Dao, enabling virtuous cycles and promoting growth："既以与人己愈多"。
5) 天之道，利而不害. Connects to Chapter 77 "天道无亲，常与善人"。Connects to Chapter 60. "其神不伤人"。

This book started out by comparing the *Dao De Jing* and the US Constitution. Its goal was to help Chinese Americans reclaim their Daoist tradition and adapt to American values.

I do not know whether I succeeded, only Time could tell.

Made in the USA
Middletown, DE
12 April 2021

37518183R00053